SUPERHERO
A BIOGRAPHY OF
CHRISTOPHER REEVE

SUPERHERO
A BIOGRAPHY OF
CHRISTOPHER REEVE

CHRIS NICKSON

ST. MARTIN'S PRESS
NEW YORK

A THOMAS DUNNE BOOK.
An imprint of St. Martin's Press.

Design by Nancy Resnick

Library of Congress Cataloging-in-Publication Data

Nickson, Chris.
    Superhero: a biography of Christopher Reeve /
    by Chris Nickson—1st ed.
       p.   cm.
    "A Thomas Dunne book."
    Includes bibliographical references.
    ISBN 0–312–19028–X
    1. Reeve, Christopher, 1952– .
    2. Actors—United States—Biography.
    3. Quadriplegics—United States—Biography.
    I. Title
    PN2287.R292N53   1998
    791.43'028'092—dc21
    [B]   98–2680

First Edition: May 1998

10 9 8 7 6 5 4 3 2 1

FOR JUNIOR
Every time I sit to type,
you are there.

ACKNOWLEDGMENTS

As always, I'm indebted to my agent, Madeleine Morel, who surely deserves a place in the agents' pantheon. Tom Dunne, my editor, has been a complete gentleman, and his assistant, Hannah Thomson, also deserves kudos. But thanks go beyond the professionals to those family and friends who offered snippets of information, advice, and plenty of support, as they always do. Without Ray and Betty Nickson, nothing would have been possible. Every time I sit down to write, I realize how much I owe you. Bob and Florence Hornberg, not just for Linda, but for keeping the cuttings coming. To friends around the globe— Thom and Tracey Atkinson, Mike Murtagh, Michael Chapman, Dennis Wilken, Jonathon and Judy Savill, Paul Clark, the members of the LUFC Internet List. Believe me, I appreciate you all. In Seattle, the marvelous Stephanie Ogle at Cinema Bookshop. Louise Oullette-Bolduc, for the translation from the French. That's the tip of the iceberg. There are others too numerous to mention, and you all know who you are.

Last, but very far from least, Linda and Graham. The love is palpable, and every bit of it is returned to you both.

Full credit, too, to the sources that have helped make this book complete. "Christopher Reeve—A Superman Who's Only

Human" by Carol Tavris (*Mademoiselle,* October 1980). "The Arts" by Jeff Rovin (*Omni,* 1980). "Christopher Reeve—Lights, Camera, Airplane" by Richard Collins (*Flying,* March 1981). "His Working Process Is More Tortured Than Mine" by Alice Kellogg (*TV Guide,* March 23, 1985). "L'Hero" by Guy Delcourt (*Starfix,* 1983). "A Down-to-Earth Actor . . . A Soaring Superstar" by Linda E. Watson (*Teen Magazine,* June 1983). "Who Fascinates Barbara Most?" by Melina Gerosa (*Ladies Home Journal,* April 1996). "We Draw Strength from Each Other" by Liz Smith (*Good Housekeeping,* June 1996). "He Will Not Be Broken" by Michelle Green (*People,* April 15, 1996). "Local Hero" by Karen S. Schneider (*People,* January 27, 1997). "Eat Your Heart Out, Lois" by Jeannie Park (*People,* April 20, 1996). "A New Direction" by Steve Daly (*Entertainment Weekly,* November 15, 1996). "Christopher's Mettle" by Steve Daly (*Entertainment Weekly,* April 11, 1997). "Christopher Reeve" by Elliott Forrest (*A&E Monthly,* October 1995). "Superman's Doctor" by Susan Reed (*People,* August 7, 1995). "The Will to Live" (*People,* June 26, 1995). "Fallen Rider" by Gregory Cerio (*People,* June 12, 1995). "A Tragic Fall for Superman" by Kendall Hamilton and Alden Cohen (*Newsweek,* June 12, 1995). "Friends, Indeed" (*People,* October 30, 1995). "Christopher Reeve" (*People,* December 25, 1995). "Woman of Steel" by Joanna Powell (*Good Housekeeping,* August 1997).

The Christopher Reeve Foundation can be contacted at PO Box 277, FDR Station, New York, NY 10150-0277.

INTRODUCTION

Christopher Reeve might have portrayed Superman in the movies, but no one had thought he might really be a superman himself. Until July 1995, that is, when he was thrown by his horse and left completely paralyzed.

For many people, that would have been the end. They'd have simply given up. For Reeve it was a new beginning, an accident that really did transform him into a superman.

To many Americans—indeed, to people around the world—he's become as symbolic in his wheelchair as he ever was in a cape. He's refused to let his disability stop him; in many ways, it's offered him a more complete and fulfilling life.

But he's always been someone driven to excel, to be the best at anything he's attempted. That's been the case from boyhood on; whether academically, as an actor, or in sports, he's always been compelled to go one step further, to push himself and expand his own limits, even if it's involved danger. So it's entirely in character that he should come to view this as another challenge to be overcome.

In the public eye, he would, and probably always will, be associated with one role: Christopher Reeve *was* Superman, the actor who'd proved to be the perfect embodiment of the superhero, who'd helped drag movies into the modern blockbuster age.

But that was as much myth as anything to be found between the covers of a comic book. The role had transformed him into a star, that much was true, but in terms of an acting career it had worked against him. It was a success he had to work very hard to live down.

By the time he was offered the part he'd already been acting professionally for a decade. The money might not have been remarkable, and his name was hardly on the tip of every tongue, but he'd learned his craft and proved himself to be very talented at it. The leading role in a big-budget film, especially one which dealt with such an archetypal American icon, was too tempting to refuse.

However fortunate it was at the time, it would become a millstone around his neck. For someone who saw himself as an actor, a person whose business was to transform himself into other people, typecasting was a terrible fate. The opportunities were there to become a major screen figure, but that held little interest for Chris. He wanted to do what he knew, what he loved—*act*. He wanted parts that were interesting, that would offer a challenge.

Challenge was what he wanted in most aspects of his life. In appearance, on the surface, he seemed perfectly conventional. He dressed like the preppy he really was, having gone to good private schools, Cornell, and Juilliard. But inside there were turbulent forces at work. *Extreme* could almost have been his watchword. From the time he was able to afford one, he'd owned his own plane, piloting himself around the country, around the globe. Skiing, cycling, horse riding. He thrived on pushing himself. Had he not been that way, there'd have been no accident. Nor would there have been Christopher Reeve.

Prior to falling from his horse, Eastern Express, on that day at Commonwealth Park in Virginia, Chris had slowly been reestablishing himself as a film actor, turning around a career that had seemed in terminal decline. But coming back so rapidly, and so strongly—even if he was still in a wheelchair, unable to move more than his head—somehow lent him a new stature and a measure of gravitas.

He's undertaken his first full directing assignment, the HBO television movie *In the Gloaming* (Chris had previously directed the second unit on one of the films he'd starred in), and his voice has been heard in any number of settings, whether on the Academy Awards, exhorting filmmakers to create better roles, at the Democratic National Convention in 1996, in hearings regarding medical insurance for Americans, or as a standard-bearer for research into spinal cord injuries.

This is the mature Christopher Reeve, enjoying the third phase of his life. The desire to do it all would have been there anyway, given his nature, but it's been heavily bolstered by his wife, Dana Morosini, their son, Will, and Matthew and Alexandra, his children from a former relationship with Gae Exton.

When he was brought into the University of Virginia Medical Center in Charlottesville, Chris had been wearing a chain around his neck with a pendant that read just "Faith." He'd always had faith in himself, and he would need it more than ever. The pendant was passed to Dana, who wore it along with his wedding ring. It was faith that bound them, and faith that would keep them moving along. And it's faith in life that's kept Chris pushing ever since.

In *Superman: The Movie* it was easy to suspend disbelief, to think that Chris really could save the world, turn back time, spend years in his Fortress of Solitude taking in the knowledge of the universe. It was easy to see in Chris's characterization the strong streak of decency that was a part of his natural makeup.

He touched people then, and if, when the lights went up,

they knew it was just a movie, many of them wanted to believe in the idea of Chris as a superman.

In the time since his accident, that's the chance he's given them. His courage and determination have made him into everything the comic-book Superman ever was, someone who refuses to accept limitations, who by his own behavior and standards has become an example and role model for others.

CHAPTER ONE

America remains a young enough country that many of its citizens feel the need for a sense of history, a background and identity, the knowledge of where their ancestors came from before appearing on these shores.

It's a connection to the past the United States alone can't offer. Most often genealogical research confirms that emigration was the only chance a family had to evade poverty, starvation, or some other type of cruel death. The poor, tired, hungry, and the huddled masses have found welcoming arms in America for more than two centuries, even if the barriers are now starting to rise.

For some, however, the past reveals surprising amounts of wealth and power. Christopher Reeve is one of those people. His bearing and patrician good looks seem to indicate a moneyed background—which he had—but it's hardly nouveau riche. The privilege dates back generations.

On his father's side, Chris can trace the lineage all the way to thirteenth-century France, where the D'Olier family was nobility, appointed to any number of lucrative offices by the kings. Inevitably, the French Revolution of the late eighteenth century made a number of changes. Many of the hereditary aristocracy lost their lives. Most others lost their titles, wealth, and land. Even those who clung on didn't have an easy time.

Chris's great-great-great-grandfather, Michel D'Olier, was born in France after the Revolution, after the Napoleonic Wars that left the country much poorer and looking for a way to climb into the nineteenth century under the Bourbon kings. As a young man he met an Irish girl and moved to her homeland, specifically county Mayo, where his son, William, was born.

If France after Napoleon had seemed like a shattered place, then Ireland in the middle of the nineteenth century must have been like one of Dante's circles of hell. The blights of the potato crop, the mass evictions by absentee landlords, and the failure of the British government to offer any real help had left the population decimated, smallholdings in ruins. Anyone who could headed west, to the land of opportunity.

William D'Olier was among them. Landing in New York with a little money, he made his way to Philadelphia. He was better off than many of the new immigrants, with some money and some skill, which he invested wisely to start the first of his cotton mills. Soon there were more, a small empire, which would bring him riches, and his heirs power.

Money bought him position in a society where the dollar was king. And it helped his children. William's son, Franklin D'Olier, became the president of Prudential Insurance during the Second World War (as well as one of the founders, and the first commander, of the American Legion).

Franklin D'Olier Reeve was Franklin's grandson, born in the family home in Philadelphia in 1928, before his parents settled in the wealthy area of Morristown, New Jersey.

Sometimes the children of fortune find themselves hating all that's been given to them on a silver platter. And that seemed to be the case of Franklin Reeve.

"He reacted against all the privilege by cutting himself off from it," Chris explained.

However, he wasn't completely without options. An extremely gifted student, by the time he parted ways from his family he already had a place at Princeton and knew that the ascetic, hermetic world of academia was where he wanted to make his future. He lived on campus, graduating in 1950 with a B.A. in English.

Franklin might have turned his back on his immediate family and their money, but that didn't mean he ignored all his relatives. One who caught his attention was Barbara Pitney Lamb, a distant cousin who had barely begun her own degree course at Vassar. In 1950, just after Franklin's graduation, they married and moved to Manhattan, where Franklin was set to begin work toward his doctorate at Columbia University.

He quickly made his name as a star student, clambering up the steps of the ivory tower. His degree might have been in English, but his real passion was Slavic, and particularly Russian, literature—hardly a field which would make him rich.

Certainly being a graduate student didn't help his bank balance, so, as well as attending school, Franklin took a variety of jobs to help support himself and Barbara—jobs that had more to do with the working than the thinking classes, as a longshoreman, a waiter, even an actor. (His political leanings were to the left, although in the early 1950s—the era of McCarthy and the HUAC hearings—that wasn't something anyone wanted to advertise.) Even living on the Upper East Side, a fairly inexpensive neighborhood in those days, making ends meet was difficult.

Barbara did what she could, penning some freelance journalism. But it wasn't too long before she had other things on her mind, discovering at the beginning of 1952 that she was pregnant.

On September 25, she presented Franklin with a son, whom they named Christopher. He was a sweet-looking boy, born with a shock of blond hair, and eyes that gradually turned blue. It spoke volumes about Franklin's academic aspirations that he asked Frank Kermode, the British scholar and writer, to be the boy's godfather.

Within a year the couple had added another child, Benjamin. For Franklin, pressured both to support his rapidly growing family and achieve his own goals, it was a difficult time. Neither was it easy for Barbara. She was just twenty, suddenly forced to squeeze every dollar and be responsible for two babies—a shock to someone who'd grown up, if not rich, then at least in very comfortable circumstances.

Inevitably, finances put strains on the marriage, which wasn't proving to be the strongest of bonds, anyway. For almost three more years the family managed to limp along from paycheck to paycheck, things gradually worsening.

The storms around them brought Chris and Ben close together. With circumstances at home so straitened, the way to lose themselves was in their imagination. Anything was grist for the mill, even boxes that had held groceries.

"To us they became ships," Chris recalled years later, "simply because we said they were."

It was impossible for the boys not to notice the way things were going between their parents. It reached a head when Chris was three, and the Reeves filed for divorce.

In the fifties most couples stayed together, even in the bleakest marital situations, "for the sake of the children." But Franklin and Barbara's union had broken down to the point where that was impossible, where hatred seemed to replace everything else, and anything was fair game to get an advantage over the other party—even using the children.

The effect on the boys was to send them even further inside themselves, to make them small, independent beings in their own minds.

"My father and mother were always fighting over me," Chris

explained, "and therefore canceled each other out. Consequently, I grew up not wanting to depend on them or anybody else. That's probably the key to my personality."

On New Year's Eve, 1956, Barbara left New York and moved back to her hometown of Princeton with the kids. While they lived with her, Franklin had visitation rights, which he exercised to the letter, making sure to drop the boys off close to—but not at—their mother's house. He wanted no personal contact with his ex-wife. They were pawns in what would be an almost fifteen-year war of silence and attrition between Franklin and Barbara.

"I felt torn between them," Chris would say in 1980. "They had a tendency to use me as a chess piece."

In the college town, the asthmatic Barbara managed to keep body and soul together for the family by continuing the journalism she'd begun in New York, this time working for the local paper, *Town Topics,* eventually becoming an editor.

It was difficult; financially things were even tighter than when she'd been with Franklin, but at least she was free to be herself again. The real casualties were the children, with Chris in particular "a solemn child," paying the price for her freedom.

Franklin had remarried, and was still living in New York, slowly working his way up the academic ladder. He would go on to have a career even more distinguished in its own way than his son's. He'd teach creative writing at Yale, then Slavic languages at Connecticut's Wesleyan University, publishing a number of novels, twelve books of poetry, and several volumes of literary criticism. He was, Chris admitted, a remarkable man, who could "do everything—from playing Parcheesi to translating Dostoyevsky."

But Franklin's world was completely circumscribed by the boundaries of the campus and the ivory tower. He knew nothing of popular culture, or the everyday world, and didn't care to know. To a young boy whose world was changing every day, and who only saw his father on the weekends, that must have made him seem distant, possibly even cold.

For Christopher and Benjamin life had quickly become complex. But it was about to become even more so. In Princeton Barbara began dating a stockbroker, Tristam Johnson, and in 1959, Barbara Pitney Lamb became Barbara Johnson.

Johnson had done well for himself, managing brokerage houses, and for the first time in their lives, the boys found themselves living with money—not only was there was no need to watch every cent, but they were surrounded by material things.

But with this luxury came a new strangeness—two younger stepbrothers, Mark and Brock, Johnson's kids—a ready-made family. (And a family of high achievers, at that: Mark is now an architect, and Brock a classicist, having studied at Yale. Allison, the daughter Barbara and Tristam would have later, has become a doctor.)

Johnson was a generous, open man, almost the opposite of the emotionally hermetic Franklin. He'd grown up in the privileged WASP traditions, and wanted—and could afford—the best for his family. But one thing he refused to allow in the house on exclusive Campleton Circle was television, which he called "the boob tube." Certainly Chris took much of the Waspish style that has always been his trademark from his stepfather. The household offered stability for Chris and Ben after the seesawing of the last few years, an atmosphere of love and laughter, of weekends away in winter, learning to ski in the Poconos, and summers on Cape Cod.

But the past had left its mark on the boys, most certainly on Chris. The patterns had already been set, not only for independence, but also in the need to excel, to be the very best at anything he undertook—a way of pleasing and getting the attention of Franklin, because he simply couldn't understand the emotional distance his real father put between them. Without a doubt, Chris put his father on a pedestal. The man had achieved a great deal, and done it all on his own abilities. The only way his son could live up to that was to be the best at anything and everything he undertook, whatever the price. When Chris was a teenager, his father taught him to sail—a passion that would remain with him—and soon had him skippering boats.

"I would win a lot," Chris remembered. "But it was at a certain cost. I would terrorize my crew. I was really aggressive, demanding, and critical of myself and other people. If I didn't win, it would set me back for days."

Johnson might have been only their stepfather, but he treated Chris and Ben just like his own kids, enrolling them in Princeton Day School, exclusive and private, where they'd be guaranteed the best education and a chance to fulfill their potential (something Ben would begin to do when he was thirteen, inventing a new computer language that would be used at Princeton University). Tests quickly established that Chris was a very bright kid, and it was even suggested that he skip a grade, until an astute school psychologist realized that putting him in a situation where he couldn't excel might be emotionally damaging to Chris, which would likely have been true.

He was musically gifted, a soprano until his voice broke, singing with the madrigal group at school. And he'd shown an early talent for the piano, which had been encouraged and enhanced by lessons. In fact, it had become a great solace to him, something he could do on his own, alone, sitting there and losing himself in the compositions, with Ravel and Debussy—notably, both quite contemplative—as his favorites. (He'd go on to become an assistant conductor of the school orchestra.)

Even though he participated in sports (he fenced and played

hockey, but steered clear of most team games), Chris tended to keep himself somewhat isolated, on the emotional sidelines. If he didn't become involved, then he couldn't be hurt. And so his interests were largely solitary, like music.

One thing he'd never considered was acting. After all, on the surface it was very much a group activity, involving the entire cast rather than the individual. And while theater might have been highly thought of in the Johnson house, the idea of actually performing had never been discussed.

Chris ended up in acting more or less through a side door. When he was in the fourth grade, and in the middle of a science class, a representative of Princeton's McCarter Theater came into the room to ask if any of the kids would be interested in taking a singing role in a production of the Gilbert and Sullivan operetta *The Yeoman of the Guard*.

Chris could sing, he had musical experience, and for reasons he never fully understood, he found himself with his arm raised. He really had no idea what to expect—his only stage experience had been with the school or church choirs, which didn't involve putting himself into any kind of character. No sooner had he begun rehearsals than he discovered that he had a taste for the theater. There was something about it that suited him perfectly: he was able to lose the rather serious boy in a costume and makeup, and become someone completely different.

"If you look at pictures of me when I was a kid, I never cracked a smile," he said in *Newsweek*. "Acting was a way to help me loosen up, expose myself, and relax."

That first production certainly seemed to turn his head, and he quickly became very active in drama at Princeton Day, almost as if he felt the need to make up for lost time; of course, involvement in that did offer a few other attractions, too: "Everyone else in school would be sitting there working on some test in third period, but I'd look at my watch and excuse myself and go to the theater."

Escaping tests and lessons was fine, but in the end it was a peripheral reason. The theater had simply captured him, in large part because "being somebody else took me away from a lot of the things I was not prepared to deal with."

His home life might have seemed perfectly settled, plenty of money, a good education, opportunities to do almost anything he wanted, but the scars of his parents' divorce remained quite raw. Indeed, that might well have been one of the reasons he attempted to do so much, simply to occupy his mind and his body, and to keep the darker thoughts at bay.

It didn't help that he'd developed into a gawky and somewhat sickly teenager, not the hunk with Superman looks who'd emerge in a few years. He'd inherited his mother's asthma and suffered from various childhood allergies. There had also been an attack of alopecia, a nervous disease which caused his hair to fall out in clumps. In his own mind, at least, Chris was still very much in the ugly duckling stage. But covered in greasepaint, he could forget about all that for a few hours, and leave real life behind.

"I was very tall and very awkward. I was six foot two by the time I was thirteen and I wasn't well coordinated. I had Osgood-Schlatter disease [a medical condition which leaves fluid in the joints, making movement a little jerky]. . . . I used to stand with my legs locked all the time, and I hated dancing."

And in 1965, hating dancing put him very much on the outside of teenage culture. The Beatles had well and truly conquered America, dragging the rest of the British Invasion in their wake. Pop music had really become the voice of a generation. Everybody danced, it seemed . . . except for Chris, and that only served to isolate him even more.

So, in that way too, the theater proved a solace. The way

he viewed himself, he wasn't about to get the girls, certainly not the ones he wanted. And being of a more earnest, academic nature, he wasn't really suited to playing the flirting game. He was just too serious.

"A lot of girls weren't ready for that," he admitted later in *Teen.* "I don't mean serious about 'I love you,' but about World War III and the latest article in *The New Statesman.* I was not a whole lot of laughs."

Being involved in production after production meant that he could avoid the problem entirely, and simply sidestep the whole dating process.

"I can remember that it solved the problem of Friday and Saturday nights. I didn't have to worry about how I was going to ask little Suzy out for a date, because I was too busy in the theater anyway."

Too busy was hardly an exaggeration. As soon as he discovered acting, it seemed to take him like a fever. After *The Yeoman of the Guard,* he took part in his first school play, *Little Mary Sunshine,* and from that point he was in virtually every school play for the rest of his time there.

"He always had the imagination, the knack for capturing an adventurous character's spirit and projecting it," was the assessment of his drama teacher, Herbert McAneny.

But Princeton Day was only able to put on one play each term, a total of three every school year, and that wasn't enough acting to satisfy Chris. He had the bug, and he needed to act as much as possible. The solution seemed to be with the group for whom he'd sung in *The Yeoman of the Guard,* the McCarter Theater.

From the time he was twelve, Chris was a regular at the theater, which was situated close to his home. From his singing role, he graduated to small dramatic parts in *The Diary of Anne Frank* and *Our Town,* and was amazed at the transformation in himself when he was acting, and the effect it had on him.

"I'm not me, I'm him. I'm the boy in *Our Town*. That got me through a lot of turmoil."

Given his sheer size, it wasn't long before Chris was taking on adult roles and beginning to realize that what he wanted in life was to make acting his career.

"I knew very early on that I wanted to be an actor," he said. "I was saved a lot of soul searching—who am I, what am I going to do with my life. Acting is what I do best."

Many parents would have discouraged such a path, since it would seem to be one full of disappointments and poverty. But Barbara and Tristam Johnson took the opposite tack—they were completely supportive of Chris's decision since it was quite apparent, as Barbara said, that "he seemed happy only when he was in a play."

The people at the McCarter Theater would play a big part in Christopher's development, not only as an actor, but also as a person. His mother and stepfather did all they could to encourage him, but it was with the group that he really began to blossom and find himself, to learn his weaknesses and his strengths and begin to accept them.

"The people I really owe my upbringing to are the repertory actors at the McCarter Theater in Princeton," he'd publicly acknowledge once he became a star. "In that atmosphere I learned to think for myself."

McCarter was a true repertory company, tackling anything and everything, from Broadway musicals to comedy to tragedy. Run by the parents of John Lithgow (the first of a number of Reeve associates who'd go on to fame and fortune), the playhouse had no set agenda beyond good entertainment. Even if an actor didn't have an onstage role, he or she was expected to help out in one way or another, sometimes in the most menial of tasks, like sweeping up. It was perfect training for those who saw drama as a career, since they'd definitely be starting at the bottom. For Chris, with his special talent, that often meant helping with the music, singing in the chorus or playing the piano—putting his other skills to good use.

Even when he was doing something as simple as that he seemed to stand out, to have a presence that made people notice him.

"I remember a director I worked under named Milton Lyon," Chris said. "I had just been in a production of *Finian's Rainbow,* which he directed. He said to me, 'You better know what you want, because you might get it. I think you might be the one in ten thousand who really has the potential to go a long, long way.' That encouraged me; handed to me at age fourteen, it made a lasting impression."

And it was bound to; at that age—possibly any age—a boy with his heart set on becoming a professional actor would eat up such praise, and it would spur him on. Not that Chris needed much encouragement, really. He already seemed completely dedicated to the theater, and pursued it as doggedly and thoroughly as everything else he attempted. He read his way through the great plays and all the books on acting he could find. The summer between his ninth and tenth grades were spent in Lawrenceville, New Jersey, studying stagecraft and makeup at the Lawrenceville School. The year after that, 1968, he spent his first summer at the Williamstown Theatre in Massachusetts, as an apprentice, more or less an assistant stage manager, doing any job that needed doing around the theater. Neither summer was particularly glamorous, but it was all part of the training, the background experiences he needed to make him into a real theatrical actor, which was the only kind of acting he considered at the time. The stage was art, and that appealed to the intellectual in him. Anything else—film, and most particularly television—was a lesser form, appealing to the lowest common denominator.

Certainly all his work paid off quite handsomely, since the next summer found him on stages all over the country. At the

Loeb Drama Center in Cambridge, Massachusetts, he had the role of Beliaev in *A Month in the Country*. From there he traveled up to Maine and performed in the Boothbay Playhouse, then rounded out the school break playing Aeneas in *Troilus and Cressida* in the San Diego Shakespeare Festival—which was enough to get him membership in Actors' Equity, the next step to making the stage his profession.

For someone who wasn't yet seventeen, it was like a dream come true. Going from coast to coast performing the classics was exactly what he wanted from life. His classmates might have gone to Europe or traveled during the vacation, but none of them could have enjoyed their time as much as he.

At the time, he was quite content to be a part of the company, paying his dues. He knew that was the way things went. And it also suited him to be one of the crowd, not particularly singled out. After hiding inside himself all through his childhood, he was still learning just who he might really be, and how this person who was Christopher Reeve could affect people.

And affect people he definitely could, at least on the stage. Once he turned seventeen Chris had an agent to handle his theatrical work. He'd been noticed and heartily approved of. However, in the Johnson family, there was no question of him graduating from high school and plunging straight into the profession, testing his fortune on the boards without a solid academic foundation. First of all he'd have to go to college.

The males of the Reeve line had been Princeton men— both Chris's father and grandfather had gone there, and it was expected that he would, too. So when he announced that he planned to attend Cornell, Franklin Reeve wasn't especially happy. Chris insisted it was because of Cornell's excellent theater arts department (although he was going to study English and music theory), but there were a number of other reasons operating below the surface.

Chris had spent virtually his whole life in Princeton. Going to college there would have offered him no new horizons; it might even have closed a few. He was at an age where he needed to go off on his own, to have a life away from home where he could be himself, free from the constraints of family. But, perhaps more importantly, choosing Cornell rather than blindly following family tradition was a way for him to assert his independence. Chris admired his father, and was certainly proud of his academic achievements, but on a more personal level there was a great deal more ambivalence. If he went to Princeton, what he did there could be directly compared to his father, just as he had been for the last eighteen years. He had a need to excel, and to earn his father's praises. Scholastically he couldn't directly compete with Franklin; hardly anyone could have. Going elsewhere he could neatly sidestep that, and begin to really become his own person.

The reasons added up, and Chris had made up his mind; no matter what was said, he wasn't about to be dissuaded. Before he could start life anew as a freshman, though, he had an acting engagement for the summer, his biggest so far, as part of the national touring company of *The Irregular Verb To Love,* with the venerable Celeste Holm in the lead role. Not only was it a major break for a young man, it was a rough-and-ready education, moving around the country for almost three months, playing the male ingenue night after night after night. It was the longest run he'd been involved with, but the repetition didn't make the magic of the theater pall. Quite the opposite; it left him even more convinced that this was what he'd been born to do.

Childhood hadn't been easy for Chris. His social skills hadn't been highly developed, and he'd never quite mastered male banter or the kind of small talk that seemed to hold girls' interest. Shyness had kept him from trying to be accepted by the crowd. But acting, the process of losing himself in someone else, had not only given him a destiny; it was, ironically, slowly forming a Christopher Reeve with confidence and a certain maturity, beginning to be comfortable with himself, and accept himself, faults and all.

He was still a fairly gawky teenager, tall, skinny, quite a physical distance from the handsome young man who'd be turning heads as Superman in a few years. His coordination had been improving (over a decade of skiing, fencing, and sailing had helped), and the Osgood-Schlatter disease that had plagued him had faded.

One thing that had remained strong was the urge to succeed at anything he undertook. To be so driven, so young, was far from a good thing, but that was simply Chris, and he'd made it work to his advantage as an actor. He'd gone after every challenge, drunk in every experience he possibly could. And he'd succeeded; to be fully professional with an agent while still a junior in high school was a remarkable achievement.

Acting in the legitimate theater was something his father, as someone who taught and wrote literature, could approve of, an important factor to Chris, who was constantly seeking his father's approval, both in his actions and his successes. Finally, having done so well and accomplished something quite concrete, he could begin to put that obsession behind him and let his sense of self, as well as his self-esteem, really develop.

He'd been lucky, spending most of his childhood surrounded by money and with parents who fully supported his theatrical leanings, even though they weren't likely to offer him either money or security. They realized, as Barbara Johnson said, that only when he was in the theater did he really come alive, and for someone so scarred by his parents' divorce that was an important consideration.

Though he was willing to satisfy everyone by putting a college degree under his belt, Chris already knew that it wouldn't change his feelings about the future. A B.A. in English might help during the lean times, but he still wanted to act. With him it had become a true vocation. And so, in September 1970 his parents drove him, and most of his worldly belongings, to the Cornell campus in Ithaca, New York. A new life was calling.

CHAPTER TWO

It was a new life, but it contained strong echoes of the old. Cornell was an Ivy League school like Princeton, the type of place Chris knew instinctively, and as a sort of straight-arrow, he fitted right in. All around him the youth movement had been going on, a social and sartorial revolution, but he had no interest in either. He was, and would remain, an archetypal preppy, wearing "khakis, button-down shirts, and crew-neck sweaters—Ivy League clothes like Princeton in the sixties."

Nor did the political furors raging all around affect him. The Vietnam War was at its height. Earlier that year, 1970, a protest at Kent State University against the war had seen four people shot dead by National Guardsmen. Much closer to home, Cornell itself was experiencing student sit-ins at its administration buildings. Turmoil seemed to fill the air.

But Chris walked through it all as if none of it was happening. His only political contribution during his time at Cornell was to help establish a dorm for acting majors.

He'd come to learn, to become rounded and acquire the polish of a degree, and he was going to get what he wanted without any distractions. He structured his time to make sure of it.

"I believe in the old-fashioned kind of education," he explained. "Studying science and math gives you the discipline to take on challenges."

Of course, he ensured there was plenty of time for theater. It might not have been his major, but it was certainly his avocation (although, in winter, there seemed to be strong competition from skiing). He socialized with the drama students; they spoke the same language, shared the same hopes and dreams. The most glaring difference was that while they remained firmly focused on student productions, Chris had his eyes very much on the outside world, taking part in professional work as his time allowed. After his freshman year he was back on the road, touring in *Forty Carats* with Eleanor Parker. All in all, it was a juggling act, working in the demands of education and the desire to be constantly treading the boards—with the boards winning easily in his heart.

"I managed to continue working as an actor during Cornell because I had an understanding agent who set up auditions around my class schedule," he said. "Somehow I managed to balance the academic and professional sides of my life."

In fact, it was the summers that really kept him going, providing his major opportunities for dramatic work. But even within his declared major, he was making theater his real focus. For one semester he managed to get leave from Cornell, with credit, to go to Europe and become a backstage observer at both the Comedie-Francaise in Paris and the Old Vic in London, two of the grandest and most celebrated of the Old World theaters. In London, he ended up doing more than observing, getting work (through his agent) as a dialect coach for a production of *The Front Page,* teaching the actors to speak with credible American accents, and also having "a grand time" wangling his way into working on "the first British production of *Equus.*"

The time away was an entire education in itself. Chris saw

how other countries looked at theater, holding it in somewhat higher esteem than most Americans, made friends and contacts that might be useful later, and accumulated more experience and a wider worldview.

Prior to his senior year at Cornell, Chris was given a rare opportunity—to become a part of the advanced drama program at the Juilliard School for Drama in New York. He possessed both the professional and academic qualifications, and his time there would build the credits to help him graduate from Cornell in 1974, after which he'd stay on to complete his second year at Juilliard.

How could he refuse? Not many people were given chances like this. Juilliard had one of the highest reputations in the country. Among the many glittering names in its faculty—someone who'd be one of Chris's teachers—was John Houseman, an actor who'd earned a towering reputation over the last half century.

And so he packed again—this time cramming his belonging into the Fiat sports car he'd bought himself with his earnings—and moved down to Manhattan.

As it turned out, Chris would be attending Juilliard at a most propitious time. Not only was he able to learn from Houseman (who'd shortly go on to a sort of television stardom in *The Paper Chase*), but his classmates proved to be a remarkably talented group—William Hurt, Kevin Kline, and Mandy Patinkin were just a few among them who'd go on to illustrious careers of their own, not to mention the man who'd be Chris's roommate, and soon one of his closest friends—Robin Williams.

As a student there, Chris became part of the Juilliard Acting Company, which presented classical drama in schools throughout New York. It gave him the chance to see just how powerful theater could be, and learn how to win over audiences that apparently had no interest in it.

"I went on tour . . . in a play by Molière called *The Love*

Cure," he recalled in a talk at the New School. "We toured some very, very heavy high schools and junior high schools in the Bronx and Staten Island and in Queens and in Bedford-Stuyvesant. We went places with our little laces and shoes and swords and funny hats, and we'd walk in there and there were some people there who would sit in the audience and would want to cause trouble and not show that they were going to be interested. Within ten minutes they were hooked. . . . They stopped moving. They got into it. They started to respond and they were taken in by Molière, who they probably never even heard of before."

It was the kind of experience that taught him a lot about his profession, and a little something about himself, and it offered food for thought, raising questions in his mind about the role of the artist.

One thing that was never in question, though, was Chris's ability. Even among such future stars, he positively shone. By now he'd spent a full decade learning his craft, but his acting qualities were, at heart, completely instinctive. Houseman recognized that and offered him fulsome praise and encouragement, tempered by the kind of pragmatism he'd soon follow himself: "Mr. Reeve, it's very important that you become a serious actor. Unless, of course, they offer you a load of money to do something else."

The first year at Juilliard sped by. He and Williams, complete opposites in personality, found themselves becoming the best of friends. Chris didn't try to keep up verbally with his roommate, who had already developed his wild style; instead he played Robin's straight man whenever he'd take off on his flights of fancy and free association. Twenty years later, after Chris's accident, stories would arise about a promise that whoever became successful first would help the other, but back then they were young men who were busy and totally focused on their work.

Chris's work at Juilliard was more than adequate for him to get his bachelor of arts degree from Cornell, although he never did make it to his graduation ceremony. The cap and gown had to remain in the closet, as he was already on tour for the summer in a play, and putting his talent to work took precedence over sitting in the sun for an afternoon and receiving a piece of paper.

At that point, circumstances meant that it had to. Chris still had a year to go at Juilliard, and that wasn't going to be cheap. His mother and stepfather had put him through Cornell, but now that he was in all ways an adult, Chris wanted to be able to make it on his own, and it wasn't going to be easy. Certainly, what he'd earned during the summer wouldn't be enough by itself. He needed something with a regular income, a "real" job if necessary, but preferably something that would allow him to make use of his talents.

The answer came from television, the medium Tristam Johnson hadn't allowed in the house when Chris was young, and one for which Chris himself didn't have much regard. Unlike most shows, the soap operas were all taped in New York, and Chris auditioned and won the role of Ben Harper on CBS's *Love of Life*.

Initially it was a small part, playing a tennis pro who was also a bigamist. Being on-screen a couple of times a week was great exposure for someone who was, to all intents and purposes, still very much an unknown, but, more important in the short term, it was also enough to pay for college and allow him to live in the kind of hand-to-mouth fashion so natural to students. And he was able to find something in the character of Harper, "if only for the challenge of making something out of bad material. In college you perform the masterpieces. It isn't like that in real life."

That was a lesson well worth remembering. Chris was already discovering the craftsman in himself.

For a few months everything went swimmingly. He taped

the show, picked up his paycheck, and still had plenty of time for his studies without stretching himself too thin. Then something he'd never imagined happened: Ben Harper clicked with the viewers. He was a bad guy, a villain, but Chris's smooth way of playing him, and his youthful good looks—even though he was still callow, there was no doubt he was handsome—made him popular. At twenty-three, Christopher Reeve was turning into a soap star.

In turn, that created problems. The writers and producers quite naturally wanted to have a popular character on more than a couple of times a week. In fact, they wanted him on-screen every day. It was impossible for him to do that and continue his studies at Juilliard.

It wasn't the "loads of money" that John Houseman had referred to a year before, but CBS was offering enough for Chris to feel that he could make a reasonable living as an actor in New York. Even if it wasn't Shakespeare or Greek tragedy, this was what he'd aspired to since *The Yeoman of the Guard*. In his mind there was really no option but to drop out of school and take his chances with the show.

Although the decision seemed cut-and-dried, it wasn't an easy choice to make. Juilliard still had a lot to offer him. He'd made plenty of friends there, with whom he could discuss the serious business of acting. And he knew there was still plenty left to learn. But Chris had been acting for over a decade, as a professional with an agent for almost half that time. He knew enough to realize the value of regular work in an actor's life, even if it was television soap opera, something quite low on the artistic scale.

He grabbed it with both hands.

The stint on *Love of Life* lasted another year, which was more than enough time to allow Chris to settle into a new life. He found an apartment, living alone for the first time on the Upper

West Side. It was small (he called it "a hole in the wall" that "looks like downtown Calcutta"), and far from what he'd been used to in Princeton, furnished as it was with castoffs, but it was a special place, his first home of his own.

What he didn't spend on his living quarters—and he spent as little as possible—went to really indulge something that had long been his secret fantasy: flying. He'd already had some lessons earlier in the year in Princeton, taught by a man named Robert Hall ("same name as the clothes guy; he is one of the real tough, grouchy, chain-smoking, coffee-drinking, nail-biting instructors who is just worth his weight in gold"). Back in New York, "I resumed flying at Teterboro Flight Academy, where I got my final polishing. . . . I took my check ride for the private [license] in that summer of 1975."

And then he put together the money he'd saved, eight thousand dollars, and bought a Cherokee 140 "with 5,000 hours on the airframe. It's a good little machine, you know. I thought, 'Hey, this is great.'"

Flying, particularly flying alone, represented the ultimate independence and freedom. Unbeholden to anyone else, he could take off and go anywhere he wanted, which he did whenever the chance or the desire occurred.

"I used to go everywhere in the little airplane and camp out," he told *Flying.* "I went to . . . Burlington, Vermont; London, Ontario; all those little towns on the way to Chicago; then down to New Orleans. I parked in grass fields every night and camped out with a sleeping bag."

For someone who'd spent much of his childhood emotionally withdrawn, being able to do all this was something of an extravagance, as far away from crowds, from everything, as he could possibly get. Chris also had something of a fascination with the *idea* of flying.

"I just love coming down after three or four hours in the

sky and being someplace else. It still amazes me. I am not yet caught up in 20th century technology."

That would happen soon enough. For now there was almost an innocence in the way he approached his life, working on the soap opera, living frugally, and pouring all his money into his new passion.

Something he was learning was that the ugly duckling he'd always felt himself to be had somehow become a fairly good-looking young swan, much to his amazement. Added to that, the "scoundrel" he played on television made him somewhat recognizable, and therefore desirable, even if it didn't always work to his advantage: Once, while Chris was quietly eating in a restaurant, a woman walked up and began hitting him with her purse, yelling, "How dare you treat your poor pregnant wife that way!"

It was the first—but very far from the last—time he'd be confused with the character he portrayed.

Mostly, though, his small celebrity worked in his favor with the opposite sex. At Princeton Day, even on the few occasions he'd tried, he'd never been able to date the girls he wanted. At Juilliard he'd been too busy. Now things were a little different. He was grown-up, handsome, and tall—Chris had ended up six feet four inches—with confidence and presence.

And this was the mid-seventies, the height of the sexual revolution, before herpes and AIDS had become widespread, when the Pill still seemed like the answer to all women's problems. It was the era when free love and the one-night stand were in full swing, and Chris had his share.

"That phase of my life was entertaining, up to a point," he'd admit five years later, "but it's also embarrassing and vaguely disappointing to wake up with someone and literally not know what she likes for breakfast. You make love and *then* try to communicate, which is all backward. I guess those experiences are part of growing up."

His character of Ben Harper might have been full of smooth lines, but Chris was still close enough to the awkward Princeton teen who'd been raised with all the social proprieties that pickup lines simply refused to float easily off his tongue. "I used to get bad attacks of cold feet," he said in *Mademoiselle*. "I found it difficult . . . to approach some girl who's sitting at a bar, minding her own business."

Somehow, the idea made him uncomfortable, even if it obviously didn't stop him entirely. It wasn't that he was on a quest for the love of his life; Chris was far too busy to have the energy for a real, involved relationship, but at the same time he found the brief flings somehow tawdry.

Love of Life paid the bills, but it didn't come close to fulfilling Chris's artistic cravings. Nor did the hurried schedule of rehearsals and tapings stretch his abilities or keep him sharp, and he quickly realized that. So he began to work with a couple of drama coaches and work during the evenings in small companies, the Circle Repertory Theater and the Manhattan Theater Club. It was all well off-Broadway, but it kept him busy, honing his skills and sating his need for "legitimate" theater.

He was still convinced that the stage was where his future lay. Television was all well and good, and movies had their place, but the stage was "real" acting.

"In film, the best movies have the most lucky moments: when the light was right, the camera was right, the makeup was right, and the horses went by at the right time. Theater, on the other hand, is a place where, through doing it again, you find out how to get past what satisfied you yesterday, and you see if maybe there is something more there. It's that process of digging for a deeper truth that is ultimately much more rewarding."

The magic that had first drawn him in hadn't palled, and,

in fact, never would. And so, when he had the opportunity to appear on Broadway—something that was more or less the pinnacle for any serious American actor—all the Ben Harpers in the world couldn't have held him back.

CHAPTER THREE

The prospect of Broadway would have been enticing enough on its own, a huge break for a twenty-three-year-old actor, even if he had already been in some seventy-five plays. But *A Matter of Gravity* was set to star Katharine Hepburn, one of the icons of American drama. That made it irresistible.

The play, by Edith Bagnold, was a comedy about self-levitation, with Chris cast as Hepburn's grandson. It was very much a supporting role, but then anything other than the lead would have been. *A Matter of Gravity* was intended to be a Hepburn vehicle pure and simple, a triumphant return.

Quite naturally, Chris was both overawed and thoroughly nervous at the prospect of working with such a legend.

"When we started rehearsals I came on like a wooden Indian. There I was, playing the grandson of a star I'd seen on screen since childhood, and the whole work process became one of trying to relax and meet her halfway."

Hepburn, with all her years of experience, had plenty of advice to give to a young actor, and was quite happy to offer it.

"She said to me, 'You must remember you are already a real person, and a real person is always more interesting than any fiction, because you exist and the piece of fiction doesn't.

So don't deny your own reality. Don't think, "Oh my God, here I am over here and there is this part over there, how am I ever going to get to it?" Assume there is a good reason you were cast in the part. Assume you have the power within you to play it. Allow yourself to say, "All right, this is me."'"

In fact, Hepburn and Reeve got along remarkably well during rehearsals. She took him under her wing, supervising aspects of his education that she felt were lacking, to try and make him into a well-rounded and presentable young man.

It was a horrifyingly busy time for him. Ben Harper was still very much in evidence on *Love of Life,* meaning that Chris was effectively working two jobs. In the mornings he'd go into the studio and record his part, before going on to play rehearsal. Once *A Matter of Gravity* went on the road, he found himself flying in from Philadelphia in the mornings for taping, until Harper was finally written out of the show.

Perhaps the most important lesson Chris learned from Hepburn in a time he'd later refer to as "my B.A. in drama" was that acting didn't have to be an obsession—it was possible to think of other things, to *live.*

"I look at her and say, 'Now here's a woman who can cope with reality. She can laugh. She can have fun. She can live. She has enthusiasm. She has outside interests. She does other things. She's a human being with capital letters and she's an actress, too.' "

But it was just one of the many things he'd pick up from her in their six months together. Chris had inevitably developed his own theories of acting, cobbled together from various teachers and ideas that just somehow seemed right to him. Kate managed to explode them all and offer him a fresh perspective.

"I'd always thought of acting as a way to lose yourself," he explained, "disappear into a part and thus find a kind of freedom. She taught me that quite the opposite is supposed to happen. You must bring your own convictions, things you really love and hate, to the character and then adjust after that."

So, for all his years of trying to escape himself, what Chris really needed to do was explore himself more deeply.

Rehearsals complete, *A Matter of Gravity* took to the road, for pre-Broadway tryouts in Philadelphia and Washington, D.C. The critics were kind to it, Hepburn being the sort of star it was almost impossible to attack. Chris found himself singled out for snippets of praise as Nicky, with the *Washington Evening Star* noting that he "makes a nice transition from playboy grandson to browbeaten husband."

Performing seemed to bring out the grande dame in Hepburn, something which had long been there, but in her old age she felt the freedom to exercise it fully. She seemed to want to take charge of everyone's life. For Chris that meant having her chauffeur drive him to various Washington museums in the morning, then lunching with her. She had her routines, and expected everyone else to fall in with them, no matter what their preferences.

"The first thing she does when she comes to the theater is open all the doors so we get some fresh air," Chris recounted. "So we breathe. She asks everyone what they'd had for dinner, and if it wasn't steak and ice cream—her idea of the essence of nutrition—you were ordered to go out and have some."

But while her attentions could become a little overpowering, there was no denying that occupying the same stage as the legendary actress was the "best unconscious acting lesson" of Chris's life.

Finally, having been tinkered with and run through, the play was ready for New York, where it opened at the Broadhurst Theater on February 3, 1976. To Chris, this was the apex of everything he'd ever wanted to do, a real high point in his life—in more ways than one.

He'd given tickets for the opening night to his mother and

stepfather—after all, it was a big occasion for them, too—and after a great deal of consideration, also sent tickets to his father and his family. For him to come and see Chris, not just on-stage but on *Broadway,* would really prove that his son had been able to accomplish something.

Barbara and Franklin hadn't spoken to each other in close to twenty years. Whether they'd say anything now and be able to keep within social conventions, or just yell, remained to be seen. But this was Chris's big night, and he wanted them to be a part of it.

"I thought, what the hell. And they buried the hatchet. Afterward we all went out and got bombed!"

That part of the evening went well. Otherwise the first night wasn't exactly a total success. Although he knew the part perfectly well, Chris was terrified before his Broadway debut, with a bad attack of first-night nerves. Hepburn advised him, " 'Now be fascinating, Christopher, now be fascinating.' I said, 'Well, that's easy for you to say. The rest of us have to work at it.' "

The vast majority of the audience was there for Katharine. Even as an older woman, she had real star quality, a true charisma as well as an incomparable acting ability, the likes of which had become rare in America.

But Chris had a few supporters of his own, some women who'd become smitten with his *Love of Life* character, which was still a recent memory, as well as some alumni of Princeton Day School, happy to cheer on one of their own. So when he made his appearance, he was greeted with a short smattering of applause. That was the type of reception usually reserved for headliners, and Hepburn, as the big name in the play, naturally noticed and "shot me a look."

A Matter of Gravity wasn't a box-office smash, by any means. The New York critics seemed to find it unsatisfying, elusive in its aims, and unfocused. The mere presence of Katharine Hepburn on a stage again was enough to keep audiences coming for a while, but the notices were hardly glowing. Where there was any praise at all, it was reserved, as it was meant to be, for Hepburn; the rest of the cast hardly warranted a mention.

But even though the major critics weren't falling over themselves in discovery of his talent, it was truly a pivotal experience for Chris. He loved, even idolized Katharine, and she, in turn, had a great deal of affection for him, calling Chris "a very sweet fellow, absolutely charming and lovely to look at. He's honest and true; you can see it in his eyes. You *believe* him."

Over the course of the run, a special relationship grew between them. She could seem like a smothering relative at times, at others coquettishly flirtatious, but she was genuinely interested in Chris, and fond of him; the two would correspond regularly for several years afterward.

"She lets me know what she thinks in no uncertain terms," he said. "She called me once to tell me about a role I had done. She didn't like the actress I was working with at all—didn't approve of her, I think was how she put it."

Being a gentleman, Chris naturally refused to name names.

But the burgeoning friendship didn't stop Kate from keeping Chris on his toes during the run of the play by inserting the occasional subtle change.

"Three performances a week I would make an entrance and get a hug and a kiss from her," he recounted to *New York Newsday*. "The rest of the performances she would raise the cane she was using to appear old, and stab me right in the solar plexus."

She was exercising her prerogative as both a star and an old woman, and thoroughly enjoying every moment of it.

The only sadness was that she was unable to exercise it for too long. After two months, *A Matter of Gravity* closed on Broadway. Even the Hepburn magic couldn't keep it alive without glittering reviews. And so the cast went their separate ways.

Chris was left in turmoil. He'd had the greatest experience

of his career, and now there was nothing. But what could he hope to do, anyway? At twenty-three he'd already been to the very top. It was as if he'd already done everything. What could be left for him in acting?

At the time it seemed impossible to believe there could be more, and the fact that the play was closing so quickly yanked his security from under him. Still young, he hadn't thought beyond it, that there'd be other parts, a whole future. It had been the be-all and end-all, his complete focus.

Depression of a sort set in, along with confusion, although his agent managed to stave it off for a little while by getting Chris his first Hollywood role, such as it was.

In *Grey Lady Down* he worked with a superior cast (Charlton Heston, Ned Beatty, Stacy Keach, and David Carradine) in one of the seventies' biggest genres—the disaster movie. Unfortunately, this didn't prove to be another *Towering Inferno*. Instead, it passed by, barely noticed, and Chris, in a small part as Officer Phillips, hardly received—or warranted—a mention, although *Playboy* did single him out for "nice work in a minor role."

When he'd finished his short stint on the movie set, Chris stayed in Los Angeles. He wasn't happy there, but there was the prospect of some television work as a lead in the television miniseries *The Captains and the Kings*. With others, he was brought in to audition, and he honestly believed the part was his. After the disappointment and deflation of a Broadway closing and a movie debut that he knew did no justice to his talents, he needed *something* meaty, a challenge of almost any kind to really bring him alive again.

The Captains and the Kings wasn't destined to be it. The lead went to Richard Jordan. Chris couldn't even do well in television now, it seemed. He began to question his ability and whether he'd made the right decision in dedicating himself to acting.

"I was twenty-four years old and being very hard on myself. I felt, I'm really not very good. I felt tense and unhappy. I went to L.A. and sat on the beach for a while. Whenever my agent tried to find me for a callback, I'd be gone. It didn't seem to matter, which is one of the signs of depression."

Gone for him meant flying, his ultimate escape, where the drudgery of everyday life couldn't reach him. Piloting gave him a great deal of satisfaction, one of the few things in his life at the time that did, given that he seemed to be in an emotional tailspin.

He also began gliding, an escape even more extreme than flying, since the sailplane had no motor, relying on air currents, thermals, and the pilot's skill to keep it aloft and in control.

Seeing just how far he could push things was about the only way he could really tell he was alive. He needed it to counter the numbness that seemed to be taking over everywhere else in his life. He didn't care about working, dating, where or how he lived.

For someone who'd been such a workaholic about his acting career, it was very worrying. As he put it, "I absolutely wrote myself off. I was sponging off friends, sleeping on couches, turning into a vegetable, and then one day I said, 'This isn't right.' "

Five months had passed, and he'd barely noticed the days going by. His family, his friends, and his agent had all been concerned. What turned him around again?

Even Chris didn't know. His attitude just seemed to change all of a sudden. There was no trigger, no revelation. He woke up one morning realizing that "you can only thrash around like that for so long. My father helped. My agent helped, and one day I was able to say to myself, 'It's time to stop flying off into the sunset.' "

One thing was certain—California hadn't been kind to him. The East Coast, especially the theaters of New York, was home to him, where he was known and felt comfortable. Besides, the stage, not the screen, was the place that felt right to him.

The time since the movie was the only period he'd been out of work in his entire career, quite an achievement in a profession where 90 percent of the participants are usually "resting" at any one time. Now, returning to his old stomping grounds was like starting afresh. He had no work lined up, and found himself regularly attending auditions.

But late in 1976 things began to go his way. He was a settled New Yorker again, and he landed a role in Corinne Jacker's play *My Life*, for the Circle Repertory Company. It wasn't Broadway, and it had no huge names like Katharine Hepburn, but that was fine with Chris. His part, as the kite-flying grandfather, offered the challenge of age and teamed him with a former Juilliard classmate, William Hurt, who had the lead. They made a good team, respectful of each other's abilities, a pair with true belief in acting (Hurt, like Chris, would continue to remain faithful to his theater roots, even as his movie career took off).

One of many plays opening and closing in New York, it didn't attract too much attention, and what it received was somewhat mixed. *Back Stage,* though, singled Chris out as "gifted and appealing."

It was satisfying work, but eighty-five dollars a week—the prevailing rate of pay—wasn't going to keep the wolf from the door, particularly as Chris hadn't worked at all since May. He needed money, and that meant doing any kind of acting work he could find. He auditioned for commercials and other theatrical parts, whatever might help his bank account stay in the black.

Like virtually every actor who'd been in a movie, Chris kept his head shots on file at the Screen Actors Guild. It was a place for casting directors to search for new faces when lining up possibilities for films. While nothing usually came of it, it was something that didn't require any work, money, or maintenance. It was one of those long shots that could occasionally pay off.

As he rehearsed *My Life,* Christopher Reeve had no idea that it would pay off in a very big way. And, beyond the financial rewards, he wouldn't have really cared. After his period in the wilderness he felt renewed, back doing the thing he loved. He'd regained his sense of perspective, that an actor's life was "You do one part and then you play another one. You finish with that one and you play another one." Some were bigger, others smaller, but you made the most of each one.

Even so, when his agent called in December 1976 and told him he'd set up a meeting with Ilya Salkind and Richard Donner, the producer and director of the much-hyped *Superman* movie, Chris wasn't thrilled. The idea of making a movie from the comic book didn't fill him with anticipation, even when he was told that he was up for the starring role—two roles, really, as Superman and Clark Kent. A serious boy, he'd never been one for reading comic books. Superman held no special place in his memory.

But work was work and money was money, and even though he strongly doubted that he'd end up with the part, he went to the meeting because "as an actor you *always* go up on appointment." Even if he didn't get the role he was auditioning for, it might eventually lead to some kind of work, something small but lucrative.

At first it didn't seem promising. Chris's photo had been picked from the Screen Actors Guild files by Lynn Stalmaster, who was in charge of casting for the film, and Salkind had liked both his look and résumé. Now, in the same room, Chris didn't seem as convincing. He was tall, but not especially muscular, and there wasn't enough maturity in his face to make anyone believe he was capable of saving the world. Still, there was enough of a resemblance to the DC Comics character to have Donner and Salkind go through the motions.

Once they asked him to offer his Clark Kent, things changed. With the help of a pair of lensless glasses, Chris immediately transformed himself into a completely different person.

"I alter my body to fit the part by controlling my spine," Chris explained later. "As Clark, I shorten myself, round my shoulders in a slouch, hold my head differently."

It was also a matter of attitude.

"Kent's attitude is 'What's going on?' . . . Clark is [Superman's] puppet."

It was enough to startle Salkind and Donner. They hurriedly arranged to have Chris flown to London, where *Superman* would be filmed, for his screen test. For a morning that had started out with just another job interview, things had got distinctly out of hand. The big question now was would the camera find him believable?

The answer came through a week later.

Superman had been discovered, and his name was Christopher Reeve.

CHAPTER FOUR

Truth to tell, Chris knew exactly why he'd been chosen for the role, and he told the *New York Post:*

"The part came to me because . . . I have the look. It's 90 per cent look. If I didn't look like the guy in the comic book, I wouldn't be here. The other 10 per cent is acting talent."

He was right, but only to a point; "the look" could only carry him so far. In his first screen moments as both Clark Kent and Superman it would be the way he looked that astounded audiences. Once those seconds had passed, however, it would be his acting skills that kept them in their seats.

The choice of Chris was pure luck, more than anything else. He was picked almost literally at the last minute, with just three months to go before filming was scheduled to begin. The actor whom the Salkinds had really wanted to portray the superhero was Robert Redford, the biggest star of the era. He knew it wasn't right for him, and he turned them down. Then they asked Paul Newman, one of the unlikeliest Supermen ever. He obviously thought so, too, and declined. After that virtually every major name in Hollywood was considered. Clint Eastwood said no. Warren Beatty, Charles Bronson, Burt Reynolds, and Ryan

O'Neal were all put forward and rejected. After that, the names became more and more unlikely, sometimes even bizarre—Ilya Salkind's wife's dentist was screen-tested.

Finally, in the middle of 1976, the producers seemed to have settled on someone—Bruce Jenner, the Olympic decathlete who seemed to represent the best American ideals. His feats (and his medals) had captured America's heart.

Had it worked, it would have been a marvelous fit, someone lithe and graceful playing the Man of Steel. But a screen test scotched that idea. On film Jenner simply wasn't convincing, or, as someone who saw his clip noted very briefly, "Jenner is not an actor."

With filming due to begin in March 1977, everyone connected with the production was becoming extremely nervous. Warner Brothers had committed $25 million to the project, while European backers had added another $15 million. The stakes were incredibly high. The Salkinds, and Richard Donner, whom they'd hired as director, needed big names, box-office draws certain to bring in the crowds. So far they had nobody.

Because of the casting difficulties, rumors were already circulating that *Superman* was in trouble, and filming hadn't even begun. Certainly there was an air of desperation starting to rise from it, which only increased when Marlon Brando was offered the outlandish sum of $3.7 million or a percentage of the gross, whichever turned out to be higher, to play Superman's Krypton father, Jor-El—a total of twelve days' work. It would make him the highest-paid actor in screen history, a distinction he wasn't about to let pass by.

Nor did Gene Hackman turn down the $2 million he was presented with to be Lex Luthor. It was looking as if *Superman: The Movie* was going to be a bonus payday for veteran actors.

What it meant was that by the time Chris signed his contract at the start of 1977, there wasn't much money left in the kitty for the ostensible star of the show. As *Variety* reported, the deal was that Chris would receive $250,000 for a full year's work (in an unusual and optimistic strategy, *Superman* and its sequel were to shoot concurrently), with $5,000 for every additional week past that. Even though it was far more than Chris had ever made, it was hardly a fortune, although Ilya Salkind seemed to feel the amount was perfectly generous.

"We're paying Chris a good salary for someone just launching a motion picture career. We want him to feel like a star. And don't forget, his salary has an escalator clause for each additional picture."

When all was said and done, there was no way Chris could turn it down. By the standards of the day, the money was more than fair, especially for an unknown. Even if he appeared on Broadway for a year, he'd never earn anything like that. Nor would he have the worldwide exposure.

"Bill Hurt, who's one of the best actors of this generation, was sharing a dressing room with me [in *My Life*] when I got that part," Chris recalled, "and he just about fell on the floor with jealousy. Any actor would have done that role."

And now the work had to begin, the real physical work of making Christopher Reeve into Superman. For the screen test, his costume had been padded. For the movie, he'd be all muscle. As much as anything, that made it a race against time. He was placed on a diet of four meals a day, and was suddenly weight-lifting three hours every day, under the supervision of British bodybuilder David Prowse, who'd provided the physical manifestation of Darth Vader in *Star Wars*.

At 188 pounds, Chris had filled out from his teenage days, but by Superman standards he remained little more than a twig. Another 30 pounds were needed, and in the right places—the chest, arms, and legs, while his waist stayed slim enough to provide the V of the comic-book hero.

"I looked at it like sketching. I was designing a body," Chris recalled, although he was really more the canvas than the artist. "I always worked looking at myself in a mirror, and not because I was in love with myself. I started out straight as a tree and gradually worked into a wedge shape, always keeping in mind that Superman had wide shoulders and no waist."

His idea of "gradually" was perhaps a little off-kilter, given that there were only three months to make the physical transformation, an extremely hectic and demanding time. When he wasn't working out, Chris had to make the preparations for his roles.

"I worked out complete makeup changes for both Clark Kent and Superman," he said. "I got old suits and bought glasses, and really practiced."

The production might have seemed to be hanging by a thread, but Chris was ready to give it all he had. And he'd given a great deal of thought to how to tackle the character.

"It's important to humanize Superman," he told Michael Petrou. "He walks through walls and can hold up the Golden Gate Bridge with his hands and so forth. So if on top of all that he said to himself, 'My God, am I good!' then you'd have a real prig, a boring piece of cardboard. . . . What makes Superman a hero is not that he has power, but that he has the wisdom and maturity to use the power wisely. From an acting point of view, that's how I approach the part."

He'd even gone to the source, Jerry Siegel and Joel Shuster, the creators of Superman, for advice. They gave him two keys: that Superman was an orphan, which "governs his emotional behavior," and the reminder that he was "an alien, and what makes him super is he's got the wisdom to use his powers well," which Chris had obviously already figured out.

He was helped by a script, which, after many changes and writers (beginning with Mario Puzo, author of *The Godfather*), ended up, in Chris's opinion, as "a romantic comedy . . . right out of a Preston Sturges movie, and the part was exactly what

I always wanted to be, a romantic leading man, a light comedian."

Even as Chris toiled away to become a Man of Steel, work was going on feverishly to complete the casting. Lois Lane was, naturally, a pivotal role, but so far she hadn't been found. Once again, the producers worked their way through a list, beginning with Barbra Streisand, and eventually, on a tip, contacting Margot Kidder.

"I saw my screen test and couldn't figure out why they cast me," she admitted later. "I played it straight, and the director was in stitches. My friends always told me I was funny, but I always thought I should be doing Russian tragedy. It's weird, because in this movie I'm showing the side of myself I reserve for friends—plus they dress me like Daffy Duck—and everyone loves it."

By the time March 1977 rolled around, it wasn't just Christopher Reeve's face and hair that looked the part. His entire body had changed. His weight had gone up a remarkable 30 pounds, to 219. He'd added three inches to his biceps, and four to his chest (bringing it to forty-five inches), and his waist was still a svelte thirty-three inches. It was, he admitted, "pure agony," but he made the character real, and physically believable. No one could claim he hadn't thrown himself wholeheartedly into the part.

Far more impressive than the measurements was the increase in his strength. The sickly, skinny child from Princeton, New Jersey, who was afflicted with asthma and allergies was now bench-pressing 350 pounds—amazing considering that he'd been straining to lift 100 pounds three months before.

The pieces were falling into place. The parts were filled, locations were set up. The crew had been hired.

There was only one thing missing. Up in the sky it wasn't a bird or a plane. Unfortunately, it wasn't exactly Superman, either.

Chris was having difficulty looking right for his flying shots. The movie's slogan would be "You'll believe a man can fly!" but at the moment that wasn't even close to the case. He was rigged into a harness and suspended in midair, often having to try to keep his body rigid *and* look natural at the same time. The wires from the harness chafed against his skin.

It took a long time for him to master it all, to come up with a technique that worked for him and also looked like a perfectly natural movement.

"Superman usually came in sideways the way a hockey player stops. But if you land from seventy-five yards in the air, it takes some practice. You come in at about the same speed as a parachute jumper."

What turned the corner for him was the realization that, more than any physical action, it was Superman's expression that conveyed the joy and freedom of flight—something he could easily understand and draw on from his own gliding and piloting experiences.

"You must see on this man's face a certain delight, a certain joy in the flying that can only come out of inner conviction."

He was even willing to take that idea one step further: "I want to convey the feeling that Superman was slightly dull on the ground, like a fish out of water. But as soon as he takes off, he's at home."

Something Chris insisted on, although he certainly didn't have to—and the producers probably dreaded it while relishing the savings—was performing all his own stunt work. Brando, for all his emulation of the Method in his acting, was horrified that anyone would do that.

To Chris, however, it seemed perfectly natural. He had the physical ability to do it. That was the first step. And doing it actually gave him more of Superman's character, made the role even more real to him. Above all, it offered him a challenge.

He wanted to push his envelope a little, to stretch himself, not just as an actor, but as a man. Skiing, sailing, flying, gliding—they were sports that pitted man against the elements, that pushed him, and Chris enjoyed being pushed and pushing back. It was a thrill, and doing the stunts offered more of that, even if some proved rather terrifying, like hanging from a crane 240 feet above New York's East River. But however frightening it was at the time, later he merely commented, with perfect aplomb, and a stiff upper lip, "I wouldn't do that again."

When it was first mooted, the planned release date for *Superman* was summer 1977. In July of that year, the cast and crew were working on location filming in Manhattan (Metropolis in the movie). There was still more location work to be done, as well as all the interiors, which would be shot at Pinewood Studios in England.

The film was seriously behind schedule, and already over budget. The politics between director Donner and the Salkinds was making everything difficult. Richard Lester, who'd worked with the Salkinds on *The Three Musketeers,* was brought in to join the team. Ostensibly his title was producer, but all his experience had been directing. He suggested that instead of shooting footage for both *Superman* and its sequel, they concentrate instead on the first movie; it was the only way the whole thing wouldn't completely collapse. Reluctantly, the Salkinds agreed.

Chris, meanwhile, was beginning to lose patience with all the infighting, which was detracting from the task in hand of actually making a film. He'd signed on to do a job to the best of his ability, to become Superman for two movies. He was an actor; the budgets and schedules weren't his concern. He had a job to do, and wanted to get on with it. What had seemed to be both an opportunity and a delight was rapidly turning into a chore.

"As far as I'm concerned, I'm finished when I've done the

sequel," he announced, stating his position and disgust quite clearly. "There may be some disagreement on the part of the producers, but the way I see it, I don't have an agreement beyond the first two."

To call *Superman* an untroubled production would be an utter lie. It was horribly over budget, tremendously behind schedule—the Salkinds had now been forced to abandon their second release date, summer 1978—and the infighting and sniping between all the powers behind the film had reached ridiculous proportions.

By the time everything moved to England's Pinewood Studios, just outside London, in the fall of '77, the most remarkable thing was that Warner Brothers hadn't just pulled the plug.

But perhaps they could sense the anticipation, the interest that all the rumors were generating. And also, they had so much money already invested that they couldn't afford to have work stopped now.

The American papers had been interested in Chris after he'd been picked for the lead, with snippets and interviews, and details of his past. But he hadn't really had a taste of being in the public eye until the British tabloids began dogging him. According to them, he was often to be found at night in Tramp's or Stringfellow's, or one of the other trendy clubs dotted around the capital.

"I'm not [in England] to have fun," Chris countered, obviously angry that someone would make him seem unprofessional. "I'm here to put something on the screen that's going to entertain people. If you go to a party on Friday, by Monday nobody remembers whether you were there or not. But they'll remember what you put on the screen whether it's good or bad. It's my job to see that it's good. . . . I go home from work each day, sometimes in agony because I feel that a scene wasn't one hundred percent. Will they fix it with music or play it off

Brando or Hackman—perhaps they'll save me. I guess I'm driven. So that's why I can't take visitors or screwing around. It drives me nuts because I'm so rigidly forward."

Perhaps it was good that he was still the driven kid who'd been captured by theater and wanted to give it his all. With everything looking like it could fall apart around him, someone needed to be focused on the task at hand. He was there for the challenge, the role, and he knew that, in many ways, the whole production depended on him. He was working with some big names—Terence Stamp, Susannah York, Gene Hackman, Marlon Brando—but it was Christopher Reeve who'd have to carry the movie. If he wasn't convincing, then the audiences would never suspend their disbelief.

"What if we miss?" he wondered. "All that work, all that money, all that care. This movie could be the biggest pratfall of the century."

That was what the producers were thinking, too, and praying wouldn't happen. At least the filming at Pinewood seemed to go relatively smoothly, and *Superman* was set to open just before Christmas 1978, a date that actually seemed possible.

As the calendar turned through 1978, it became make-or-break time, and Warners did everything to ensure it was make. The advertising budget for the film was $10 million, an unbelievable amount for the time. But the era of the blockbuster had been ushered in. First there'd been *Jaws,* then *Star Wars* and *Close Encounters of the Third Kind,* each upping the ante in box-office numbers, grosses, and special effects. More than any other movie opening in the same season, those films were *Superman's* real competition, the standard it would have to beat.

The very first British "public" screening wasn't exactly public. On December 13, 1978, *Superman* was the royal command performance film in London, with Queen Elizabeth II as the main guest, and Chris, as the star, was presented to her. It was by invitation only, with no reviewers present to proffer their comments.

Three days earlier the American premiere had taken place in Washington, D.C., and Chris had been on display there, too. It was a benefit for the Special Olympics and the roster of names positively glittered: President Jimmy Carter and his wife, any number of politicians, Henry Kissinger, Barbara Walters, even news anchor Roger Mudd.

Becoming Superman hadn't just put Chris in exalted company, it had also made him into a very public figure. After so much work on the movie, the suddenness of the attention left him a little uncomfortable. He'd become a commodity rather than a person; never again could he be just Christopher Reeve, actor, although that had yet to fully sink in. When reporters asked him how it felt to be a movie star, the only honest answer he could give was, "I don't know. This is only the third day I've been one. Come back in a year and I'll tell you."

In some ways the round of premieres and gala openings was almost more grueling than the filming schedule. The following day found Chris in New York for a second American premiere, with its own gala set of politicians and celebrities. And it hadn't even opened in theaters yet; that was still four days away, on December 15.

The movie was divided into three parts. It began with the destruction of Krypton, as predicted by Jor-El, and the tale of how he sent his son to Earth, the only survivor of his race. Then there was the young Clark Kent, who might have looked like the archetypal ninety-eight-pound weakling, but who had already discovered some of his amazing powers and was frustrated at not being able to use them.

And finally there was Superman proper, who didn't appear until the movie was almost halfway done. From Chris's entry the film took off, both literally and metaphorically. Up to that point it had been slow, and, in Brando's sections, even turgid and pompous. But as both Clark Kent and the Man of Steel, Chris brought a very light touch to the character. There was an obvious, believable spark between him and Margot Kidder (even if it only existed on the screen), while Gene Hackman, Ned Beatty, and Valerie Perrine hammed it up as the crooks. It was, as Chris had predicted, a romantic comedy, in the very best sense.

Of course, there were also the special effects. By the standards of the 1990s they seem quite crude, often jerky, but for the time they were something of a revelation. Yes, you did believe a man could fly, and hold up a helicopter, or even repair the San Andreas Fault and turn back time. The linchpin was Chris. All his work had really paid off. His flying and landings looked completely natural and realistic. And because he'd done his own stunts, the cameras could zoom in on him in action. Going that extra yard helped give punch to the production.

Even before the public had a chance to see it, the critics were offering their opinions. While some thought the overall pacing was erratic, most loved it. And how could they not? Two years after the bicentennial, this was a perfect little slice of Americana, full of Mom and apple pie, "truth, justice, and the American way," even as it offered sly little winks at convention. In the end all the wrangling had more or less been worthwhile. The *New York Daily News* summed it up as "pure escape and good, clean, unadulterated fun."

Inevitably, as the centerpiece, Chris was a focus for comment. But he most certainly wasn't found lacking. In *Newsweek,* Jack Kroll wrote that his "entire performance is a delight. Ridiculously good-looking, with a face as sharp and strong as an ax-blade, his bumbling, fumbling Clark Kent and omnipotent Superman are simply two styles of gallantry and innocence." Pauline Kael, writing in *The New Yorker,* found him to be "the best reason to see the movie. He has an open-faced, deadpan style that's just right for a windup hero. Reeve plays innocent, but not dumb, and the combination of his Popeye jawline and physique with his unassuming manner makes him immediately likeable. In this role, Reeve comes close to being a living equivalent of comic-strip art."

The verdicts were in, and Chris was a winner. But the real test came with the public. The writers could churn out whatever copy they wanted, and praise the film to the skies, but if people weren't prepared to open their wallets, it was a flop.

So on December 15, 1978, there was still plenty of tension in the *Superman* camp. After all the work and the advertising, would it be a hit?

Probably the only one not biting his nails was Chris. He was at the Cooper Union Forum in Manhattan, hosting a concert of works by Vivaldi, Mozart, and Liszt. He had, after all, once been quite serious about music himself, and it had remained an important part of his introspective side. He'd done everything he could to make *Superman* a success, and had given it, in the end, eighteen months of his life. After that, even through the growing onslaught of publicity, he needed some time for himself.

Part of that meant getting away, far away, from the crowds and the hurly-burly of life. Although he couldn't quite afford a yacht of his own yet, Chris had devised a scheme that managed to get him on the ocean at no cost—he did yacht deliveries. Recently, in return for airfare, meals, and drink, Superman and a crew had sailed a businessman's boat from Toronto to Bermuda. All work and no play could make Chris a very dull boy, and there'd been far too much work lately. Like the music, it was something he needed for his mental health.

And he was going to need that even more. Because, whether he wanted it or not, Christopher Reeve was now a bona-fide movie star. Opening in seven hundred theaters across the country, *Superman* grossed a staggering $12 million during its first week alone. That was the largest amount any film had taken in during the week before Christmas, and only the first of many motion-picture records it would go on to break. It had the highest attendance records for *any* holiday period, and would soon become one of the highest-grossing movies ever made, taking in a total of more than $300 million around the world.

Superman and some other films of the time showed it was possible to be both a blockbuster and a "good" film, with content well above the lowest common denominator, and they were duly rewarded. The National Board of Review named *Superman: The Movie* one of the Ten Best Films of 1978, and it received four Oscar nominations—Best Film Editing, Best Sound, Best Original Score, and Best Visual Effects (for which it would win its sole Academy Award). Chris was bypassed, as was the rest of the cast, but Britain, at least, seemed to sense the potential in his performance, giving him a BAFTA (the English version of an Oscar) as Most Promising Newcomer, an award which had been won the year before by Emma Thompson.

It wasn't the only trophy to grace his mantelpiece. The U.S. Junior Chamber of Commerce named Chris one of their Top Ten Young Men of the Year, which might have seemed slightly odd, until the explanation was given—for his work in "helping young boys deal with the trauma of a broken home," something he certainly knew from personal experience. In his interviews, Chris had been quite candid about his own background, the effect it had on him, and how he'd overcome it. Through his honesty, he'd inadvertently become a symbol to a growing percentage of the population.

Although he wasn't in contention, Chris's new stature in the business more or less demanded that he attend the Oscar ceremony. The show over, most of the celebrities off to their parties, and the cameras packed away, he found himself backstage with Cary Grant and John Wayne. All three, in their separate ways, were icons of Americana, with Chris decidedly the new kid on the block. Wayne certainly seemed to accept him into the club. As the introductions were made, he said to Grant, "This is our new man."

It was a story that Chris would repeat endlessly, and with glee. After all, not everyone was accepted by the Duke as an equal.

To the audiences who crowded into theaters all over America, Christopher Reeve simply *was* Superman. It was a testament to his acting ability that the association was so immediate and so strong. At the time it seemed wonderful, if a little daunting, as he became flooded with piles of fan mail.

"You would not *believe* what women would expect from somebody who played Superman," he told *Mademoiselle*. "I'll just leave that *entirely* to your imagination!"

There were also the inevitable countless requests for publicity appearances. Chris thought he'd learned something of the power of a character when he'd played Ben Harper on the soaps, but that was absolutely nothing compared to the interest shown in Superman. Some of the things, he was more than happy to do, like talking to kids about his character.

"They should be looking for Superman's qualities," he explained, "courage, determination, modesty, humor—in themselves, rather than passively sitting back, gaping slack-jawed at this terrific guy in boots."

Being a hero and a star, he quickly learned, involved responsibilities that extended well beyond the film itself.

"It's very hard for me to be silly about Superman, because I've seen firsthand how he actually transforms people's lives. I have seen children dying of brain tumors who wanted as their last request to talk to me, and have gone to their graves with a peace brought on by knowing that their belief in this kind of character is intact. I've seen that Superman really matters. It's not Superman the tongue-in-cheek cartoon character they're connecting with; they're connecting with something very basic:

the ability to overcome obstacles, the ability to persevere, the ability to understand difficulty and to turn your back on it."

And Chris was the kind of person who took his responsibilities seriously. All this was new to him, and he wanted to do it, as he did everything, to the very best of his ability. He'd plunged into the publicity machine and discovered he was very welcome because he was voluble, charming, and articulate, a rare combination in an actor, and rarer still in a movie star. He was concerned with his work, not his image. He was Superman, and for now that suited him very well. It never occurred to him that he'd end up completely typecast in the public eye as the Man of Steel, and that what seemed like a luxurious liberation would end up being a trap.

Immediately, though, there was no reason for him to think that the cape of a superhero would end up being a millstone around his neck. Chris's experience was in the theater, where that simply didn't happen. He might be a movie star, but he was very much a novice in that game. In his world you moved from one part to the next. You performed and moved on. Granted, in film some people managed to avoid it. Harrison Ford, for example, evaded Han Solo, even though he played the character in three films. But Han wasn't the central character—Luke Skywalker was, and Mark Hamill was never able to leave him behind. For most screen actors, that was the case. Sean Connery, and to a lesser extent Roger Moore, will forever be associated with James Bond. Michael Keaton managed to avoid being dogged by Batman largely because the hero was always masked, and because he'd already established a strong movie career beforehand.

Chris was playing something more than just a known quantity. In America, indeed throughout the world, Superman was an icon, a symbol both of the first golden age of comic books and of America itself (and the two were intertwined, comic books being so peculiarly American). In a way, that made Chris an American ambassador of sorts. *He* was the focus of the film. Even though he appeared for little more than half the running time, the earlier part was merely prologue; nothing really happened until he came on-screen. And he wasn't in a spaceship or on some alien landscape. This was quite recognizably Earth, specifically New York, in the present day. There was no mask—as Superman or Clark Kent, we saw *him*. Finally, of course, the film was phenomenally successful. After being seen by so many people, and so widely praised, it would have been almost impossible to have not been typecast to a degree.

For now, though, with *Superman* breaking every box-office record in the book, Chris was being deluged with scripts. He was young, handsome, and hot, and everyone wanted him.

He could have had his pick of virtually any project, but that was one thing he didn't want. Having this Hollywood clout, he thought, should be a freedom, rather than a restriction. He should be able to do what *he* wanted, rather than follow the prescribed path for up-and-coming stars. He wanted to work with "the Varsity: Alan Pakula, Sidney Pollack, Lumet, Michael Apted, Ritchie—that gang—Arthur Hiller, Colin Higgins. I want to work with the pros, the top team of experienced people—David Lean, George Cukor. I like the old masters."

It was an impressive list of names, and it showed that Chris knew exactly who the classy filmmakers were, that he'd studied the art, just as he'd taken the time to study everything he was involved in. But Hollywood was on a cusp. These people were the old school, and it was the new school—Spielberg, Lucas, and others—who were making the films everyone wanted to see. The studios were throwing money at them. It was the dawn of the age of special effect as star, where the $40 million spent on *Superman* would end up seeming like small potatoes indeed.

Chris was in a position to pick what he wanted to do next, and he was determined to make a careful choice, to end up with something that truly appealed to him, rather than simply grab the big-money roles. That in itself showed an adventurous spirit, a willingness to walk away from the yellow-brick road.

He turned down *Urban Cowboy,* and then refused what was, literally, a $1 million offer to star in *American Gigolo* for the moral and pleasingly old-fashioned reason that "I found the idea of a man servicing older women for money quite distasteful."

Then there was *Body Heat,* which he bypassed.

"I didn't think I'd be convincing as a seedy lawyer," he explained. Instead the part went to his friend William Hurt, his second major film role.

This was Christopher Reeve as a man of staunch principle. The part was far more important than the money.

Needless to say, his agent wasn't happy to see him walking away from any number of open gold mines. But Chris knew what he wanted, and it was something he'd stated before, picturing himself as more of a romantic leading man. He explained it to the *Detroit News:* "They've had an awful lot of brooding leading men—complex, secretive characters played by guys like De Niro, Hoffman, Pacino. I suppose I can offer a simpler alternative."

In a film world where the lines between the good guys and the bad guys were becoming very blurred, Chris wanted to hark back to a more innocent age, where you knew who was who, and what was what. The only problem was that they weren't making big films like that any more. In the late 1970s there wasn't much call for Jimmy Stewart–type characters.

Meanwhile, Chris's name was still being associated with a number of projects. *Dink Stover at Yale* didn't sound particularly promising, and soon vanished into the mist, never to be heard of again, as did many of the others.

A lot of people were beginning to wonder just what it would take to excite Chris. He was still hot, but in Hollywood people can cool off very quickly. If he was going to maintain his status as a movie star, he needed to strike soon, and in a project with a big budget and plenty of visibility.

He struck, but what he plumped for was a film that had neither a lot of money nor a great deal of visibility. When he finally put his name on the dotted line, it was for another half a million dollars to star in *Somewhere in Time,* an adaptation of Richard Matheson's novel *Bid Time Return.*

The entire budget for the film was $4 million (which would eventually rise to $6 million). This wasn't something with blockbuster written all over it, and that suited Chris perfectly. It was his chance to "escape the cape."

CHAPTER FIVE

While Chris now had the opportunity to see his professional life blossom, on a personal level he was becoming far more focused, and he had Superman to thank for that, too.

His days of haunting Manhattan's singles bars and waking up with women whose names he didn't know were now behind him, just as he was coming into his own as a sex symbol. For now Chris had a real established girlfriend, the first relationship he'd enjoyed that had lasted more than a few months. He'd been smitten on the odd occasion before, but this, beyond any doubt, was the real thing.

Her name was Gae Exton, and he'd met her at Pinewood Studios. He had, quite literally, bumped into her at the studio commissary. In costume (as Superman, and amazingly not as Clark Kent) he'd stepped back from the counter backward and trodden on her toe.

It wasn't the most auspicious first encounter.

"She just thought I was a large American person with black hair and wore red boots," he recalled. While she didn't seem overly impressed with his appearance, he couldn't quite get her out of his mind. So it was serendipity when they met again a few weeks later. This time Gae managed to emerge without injury. But she did walk away with something else—a date with Chris.

Like a lot of women, she found him attractive, partly for those blue eyes of his. But she was quite adamant that "it wasn't love at first sight."

Gae Exton was an ambitious woman. She always had been. Just a few months older than Chris, she'd already done a lot with her life. Growing up every bit as resolutely middle-class as Chris, after convent school she'd worked in the restaurants her father owned, before opening her own place when she was just twenty-one.

Not content with that, on the side she'd also had a moderately successful modeling career. For a kid who'd been even more sickly than Chris, in and out of hospitals until she was a teenager, she'd developed a huge amount of drive and energy.

After a while Gae had had enough of the camera, and decided to apply her management skills and model contacts to running a modeling and casting agency in London. The day she met Chris she'd been at Pinewood talking to casting directors for various television shows.

Unlike Chris, she wasn't exactly single when they met. In fact, Chris noted, emotionally she "was fragile as an eggshell when we met." Her marriage to David Iverson had collapsed, and the couple had only recently separated. Iverson had come up from the working classes, a coal miner who'd remade himself as a businessman before finally turning to crime (in 1979 he'd be sentenced to three years in prison for cocaine smuggling). The last thing Gae was looking for in her life was a new relationship, a romantic involvement.

Nonetheless, she went out with Chris. Their first date took place on October 16, 1977 (Chris, showing a strong romantic side, would refer to their first date as "our anniversary" with both Gae and later with Dana Morosini), when he took her to see *The Belle of Amherst* starring Julie Harris, playing on Shaftesbury Avenue in the West End—London's equivalent of Broadway—before they went on to enjoy a quiet dinner.

By the end of the evening Gae knew she liked Chris, a feeling that petrified her. She knew where it could lead, and she just wasn't ready to deal with that.

"I didn't want him to kiss me. I was scared of my physical attraction to him. . . . I jumped out of the taxi, shouted, 'Bye!' and ran away. The first kiss didn't take place until the third date."

Wary she might well have been, but the attraction was strong enough that she didn't turn him down when he asked her out again . . . and again. Chris had to dismantle her defenses, and he did it slowly and carefully, being every inch the gentleman.

"She was shocked that I wasn't going to muscle past the door into her bed. I think the fact that we tiptoed into the relationship helped."

Prior to Gae, Chris's girlfriends had all been actresses, as much a part of the theater as he was. While those relationships can, and have, worked for some, it takes two remarkable people to thrive together in such a hermetic world. For most it's a recipe for disaster. Gae's connection to the business was peripheral. Even if she saw the same things as Chris, her perspective was utterly different, that of an outsider. There was no inherent sense of competition between them.

And that meant Chris could relax around her, "let go" as he put it. She was quite successful in her own right, established in her profession, so she wouldn't simply be an adjunct to him, the little woman on his arm.

Once Gae's wariness had finally worn off, and she relaxed too, she quickly found herself falling for Chris. It was completely mutual; he was crazy about her. Four months after their first date he moved into her apartment in Knightsbridge, right in the heart of London.

It was a major step for both of them. Chris had never lived

with anyone before—he'd never had a relationship that had been anywhere near as serious. And for Gae to let someone become so close so soon after her marriage showed just how deeply she felt, that she was willing to risk all this. It was love, true love.

Initially there was no question of them marrying, in large part because Gae was still legally married to David Iverson. More than that, however, neither of them felt the need to have a wedding ring keeping them together.

Some people thought that the reluctance to marry was all on Chris's part, that the divorce his parents had gone through when he was young had left him somehow scarred and afraid to make that same commitment himself. But he wasn't about to give credence to thoughts like that.

"It's true that I was the product of a certain polarity in a divorcing family," he explained in *Cosmopolitan*, "but I refuse to trace my attitude back to my parents. That's a sixty-five-dollar-an-hour question."

However, one thing he felt no need to do was parade his romance in public. He might be getting plenty of attention for the role he was playing in *Superman*, but this was his private life, and he was determined to keep the two separate.

For her part, Gae saw no need to have legal ties to someone she shared her life and love with. She'd done it once and been burned; there was no call to repeat the mistake. She was a strong, independent woman, not threatened or intimidated by Chris's impending stardom.

"That was one of the things that attracted me to her," Chris said. "She was and is singularly unimpressed by celebrities. You're a movie star? Fine. A shoe salesman? Fine. That quality is very attractive to me, because you know you have to sink or swim on your own personality."

She was certainly his rock and his touchstone with reality as the hype about the movie grew during 1978. Without even trying, Chris was becoming famous. He and Gae went out together, but privately—to dinner, the theater, dancing. And that was a good thing, since it gave the relationship a chance to grow and develop away from the spotlight. By the time they made their first public performance they'd been together for a year. But when they revealed themselves publicly as a couple, it was in the very highest style, when *Superman* was screened for Queen Elizabeth, and Chris got to introduce Gae to Her Majesty.

Even for such an occasion, Chris was reluctant to subject Gae to scrutiny.

"I'm going to have to be a public person, but I was keen on Gae not becoming a household name, because then we could lose what we have."

Interestingly, the part of their relationship which came under the microscope more than any other was the fact that they lived together without being married. In England it hardly raised an eyebrow, but the American press frequently brought it up as a topic. In the United States, of course, it was deemed fine to marry and divorce frequently, but to "live in sin" was somehow morally reprehensible, and certainly something Superman would never have done. It forced Chris into a corner, having to defend the way he and Gae had chosen to live their lives, rather than having people just accept them as a couple.

"I'm not advocating our solution to the general public," he found himself almost apologizing, "but it works for us. We are as married as any couple in America. We are absolutely together and faithful to each other, but I appreciate Gae more when I don't have her locked up and filed under 'G.' . . . Our feelings are still growing and changing. We have a commitment, yet with an improvisational quality to it that keeps it alive."

That it should even have been commented on showed a great deal of hypocrisy on the part of the press, but in the late seventies the whole idea of "alternative lifestyles" and "living together" still smacked very heavily of the hippie days of free love, drugs, and social anarchy.

In retrospect it seems more than a little over-the-top, if not completely ridiculous. But at that time, and to a lot of people, particularly in Middle America, it was a contentious issue, and one that brought about even more debate once Gae became pregnant in 1979.

It was unplanned, but still completely wanted. Once the news leaked out—inevitably, after a while it was impossible not to notice Gae was pregnant—the questions, which had eventually died down, started anew.

"Having been married once, I'm in no hurry to do it again," Gae said. "Chris and I have an excellent relationship the way it is, and we don't want to change it. We're a couple in everybody's eyes—I think most people forget we're not married."

In the end, what did it matter, anyway? Married or not, they were together, they were happy, in love. Living together without benefit of clergy was hardly something new or even that radical. In terms of their generation, it was quite common, virtually normal. The "problem," if there really was one, was just in the eyes of the beholders.

The era of the two-career couple had begun, and Chris and Gae were quite definitely part of it. So she tended her business in London when he went off to film *Somewhere in Time* in 1978.

The location, while not as exotic as he'd have had if he'd accepted some of his other offers, was still unusual—Mackinac Island, in Michigan.

It was a place that presented logistical problems for crew and cast, in large part because no cars were allowed on the island (although a dispensation was granted for the vehicles used in the film). Transportation was either by horse or bicycle, neither of which was conducive to moving heavy film equipment or film actors more used to being driven in limousines.

Nonetheless, the producers had decided this was the ideal place to film a sweeping romantic drama. Chris found himself working opposite Jane Seymour, a British actress who'd first become noticed as a Bond girl, one of 007's many lovers (she had been in *Live and Let Die*). She was still really waiting for her career to take off, little suspecting that her real future would be in television.

There were plenty of naysayers who were still predicting that this would be a big mistake for Chris, that he needed something with a great deal more visibility (not to mention money).

"My team told me not to take the part," he admitted in the *New York Times.* "They said I should only do a movie directed by Michael Cimino. It should be opposite Jane Fonda or Barbra Streisand. But I like the character—a man who's incomplete. He has all the material things he needs, all the comforts, but he's missing a passionate commitment to something other than himself, and goes in search of it."

Granted, the whole action Chris took was something of a reaction to the commercialism of *Superman,* with its tie-in lunch boxes, action figures, and every other possible piece of merchandising—the Salkinds were soaking it for every penny. His portrayal of the Man Of Steel might have been wonderful, but somehow the innocence had ended up being a little lost and irrelevant in the hoopla and hype of the franchise. *Somewhere in Time* would offer him a chance to shine, to be more himself (and he most definitely was a romantic at heart). It was, he said, "an absolutely honest attempt to create an old-fashioned romance. It's based on love rather than on sex or X-rated bedroom scenes."

The role of Richard Collier, the man who'd achieved material fortune in the contemporary world, "allowed me to crawl into a man's head, to nurture what is still emotionally alive in him. It's about a successful man who is half-dead inside—until he sees a portrait of a woman who lived nearly seventy years before. At this point the film becomes a study of how desire can affect someone. He goes to see this woman, travels back in time through a mixture of inducement and suggestion, and creates a period environment around himself so convincing that after three days of trying he just leaves. In essence, *Somewhere in Time* is about a man looking for one from the heart."

And Mackinac Island, with its very strong turn-of-the-century period flavor, was possibly the perfect place to find the film's atmosphere. What no one had reckoned on was the fact the Chris was allergic to the island's ubiquitous horses. He survived by using a bicycle and taking allergy pills for the duration of the shooting. Even so, there were times when his eyes would water and his nose would run, not exactly the suave qualities of a leading man.

But then again, Chris was a very human leading man, even if he'd made his movie name playing an alien. And as such, he had all the human failings, including clumsiness. Dancing with Seymour, he found himself standing on her foot more than once, which earned him the endearing nickname of "Superfoot."

One of the big disadvantages of being trapped on an island was that it made Chris a sitting target for the many fans who wanted to see Superman in the flesh. Mackinac had long been something of a Michigan tourist mecca, and the rumor that Chris was there filming brought plenty of people onto the island's ferry. All that was good for business, but very disruptive for *Somewhere in Time,* as the crowds ended up hampering the shooting schedule. It finally reached the point where Chris was forced to make an agreement with fans. If they'd let him work in peace, when everything was finished he'd tour the state and sign autographs.

Really, it was a sign of just how popular Chris was—and more to the point, just how huge *Superman* was—that the fans would stream in to see him that way. It was a given that a movie star would receive fan mail and adulation, but for someone with only one starring role under his belt, this was quite re-markable, almost unprecedented.

However, the times they were definitely a-changin', and Chris represented a new breed of man. The old school had been macho and manly, always strong. They were the heroes of black and white, in more ways than one.

But even when he was showing superhuman prowess at fighting crime, Chris's character let his sensitive side come through. There was an innate courtliness to his behavior that seemed to go beyond any script and emanate directly from Chris himself, which was guaranteed to appeal to women.

And it was perfectly true; he was like that in real life (which helped him bring such natural truth to Collier). Unlike so many who'd gone before, he came across in three dimensions, not just a handsome face and a set of muscles. Intelligence flick-ered in his eyes. He was thoughtful and articulate when inter-viewed, speaking in grammatical sentences. There was none of the ruggedness about him. Instead, he was decidedly clean-cut, and with his wardrobe—still big on the preppy basics—and rather earnest manner, he could have been a graduate student or a young professor.

All of that was perfectly in tune with the times. Fashion had changed, leaving the old order standing at the roadside. Peo-ple still wanted to be able to look up at their stars, but they also wanted the person on the pedestal to be an idealized re-flection of themselves, rather than someone completely un-touchable. And Chris filled the bill.

He found it all faintly ridiculous, however. He didn't think of himself as a movie star, and never would, at least in the ac-cepted sense. He saw himself as an actor who'd had a particu-larly lucky break, nothing more or less. Outside of the roles he was creating, to Chris his looks and manner were irrelevant to anyone but himself or Gae.

In his eyes, each part he played, whether great or small,

had equal value. He was like other actors in that "We're not putting value judgments on the character. We're not saying a comic book is worse than Chekhov. It's all the same process to get inside and believe it."

So that he should have become the object of screams, lust, and fantasy for doing his job was dumbfounding, even embarrassing, since he was being singled out for his looks and his style, neither of which had that much to do with his acting ability.

His biggest concession to his new status was a new airplane—he'd moved up from the Cherokee to a new A36 Bonanza, and now, having completed his multiengine rating, he'd added a Beech Baron to what was almost becoming (and would soon actually become) a little airline. They were his toys and his escape valve.

And, more importantly, he had a new home. In London, he and Gae lived at her Knightsbridge apartment. But in New York they didn't have a decent place. The old bachelor pad wasn't exactly suitable for a couple. So now that he had the money, Chris bought a penthouse in a co-op building, still on the Upper West Side, on West Seventy-eighth Street. It was elegant, swank, and not cheap. Still, he reasoned, he had the money; he could afford the indulgence. And real estate would only rise in value.

But those were simply the trappings that money had brought. At heart he hadn't changed at all. For someone who viewed himself as a movie star, *Somewhere in Time* would have been a bad career move. For an actor, it made perfect sense to show another facet of his abilities.

With its element of time travel it was no less fantastic than *Superman,* and Chris himself admitted to film critic Gene Siskel, "I'm sure there will be cynics in the audience who say, 'Oh, come on, this is ridiculous.' But those are the same people who think that Heidi is a little pain in the ass who is forever yodeling, and that the kids in *The Sound of Music* should have been drowned at the beginning of the picture."

It was definitely a tearjerker; but that was the whole intention. It was, in the Hollywood scheme of things, a small movie. But it came in on budget (the crew had been asked to take a pay cut so the production could afford Chris) and on time. Shooting didn't take long (for which a highly allergic Chris was grateful).

How would audiences react? After seeing Chris in a cape and red boots, would they be willing to accept him as a writer moved by love? For that matter, had the world moved so far from innocence that an unabashed weepie would seem stupid and totally outdated? When it opened in 1980 the verdict soon became apparent.

It was a subject that needed a light touch to work and glide, and director Jeannot Swarcz instead applied a rather heavy hand. He'd done a good job with *Jaws II;* however, that was action, and this was anything but. In fact, that was a big part of the problem—it was *too* static.

Chris would say later that he "overacted dreadfully," and he certainly did, but the air of Mackinac seemed to affect the whole cast in the same manner. There wasn't a single person who didn't go way, way over the top.

As the object of Richard Collier's desire, Jane Seymour had a nice smile and plenty of hair, but that was about as far as praise could go. She was by no means a great actress, in fact not even a good one.

Christopher Plummer, as her manager, was assured and suave, even as he hammed it up. It was almost as if everyone involved found it impossible to take the film seriously.

But while it edged toward self-parody, it never developed a human edge. The earnestness always showed through, most of all in Chris, who was, after all, the focal point. Subtlety should have been the watchword, but it was somehow forgotten.

Most critics hated the film—and Chris in it. The goodwill he'd built up in *Superman* didn't carry over to this. In the *New*

York Times Vincent Canby gave an honest appraisal of Chris's performance, saying that "unfortunately, his unshadowed good looks, granite profile, bright naivete and eagerness to please—the qualities that made him such an ideal Superman—look absurd here."

And it was true. Chris still looked too young, as if he hadn't lived and suffered yet. Richard Collier was supposed to be a successful man full of Weltschmerz, but without the haggard look of worry, it was hard for Chris to put that across. At least *Variety* came to his defense, one of the very few publications that liked the film, praising him as "a fine actor with both star power and versatility . . . a first-rate and exciting romantic lead, able to handle both comedy and drama with equal skill."

On the heels of the reviews, *Somewhere in Time* didn't do a great deal of box-office business when it was released. For a film that had been so eagerly awaited, the second big outing for the man who was such a smash hit, it more or less died on the vine. However, the irony was that it refused to go away. A core group of people loved it, and through video rentals many more continued to discover it. While never enough to make it a hit, the movie remained known and popular, to the extent that it had its own fan club and even its own Web site on the Internet. Whereas virtually every other movie from the time has been forgotten, it's stayed alive, in a rather bizarre echo of the plot.

For Chris it had been a mistake, really, but an honest one that could still be absorbed and corrected. He was still a desirable movie property. With *Superman* the pendulum had swung very much to one side, and in reaction Chris had gone to the other extreme. What he needed was to find a middle course.

On top of that, it was really only his second movie role (discounting the bit part in *Grey Lady Down*), and he was still finding his feet in the medium. His time in the theater had shown that he could act, but movies were a very different beast from the stage.

"In a movie, you've got the money problem, you've got the producer problem, you've got the studio," he'd muse a few years later, "and the fact that they only keep you there for the minimum time they possibly can because they don't want to pay the money. You do a scene and the girl who plays your wife, you met her yesterday. It's very hard to bring out any depth. But in theater, what comes out is the collective, the group."

Chris might have leapt tall star ratings in a single bound, but he was still learning, and he knew it. He'd been helped by the fact that *Superman,* for all its problems, had been thoroughly professional in its scripting. For *Somewhere in Time,* Richard Matheson had written both novel and screenplay. He was experienced, but all his previous work had been in the general horror field—movies with titles like *Die! Die! My Darling* and *Master of the World,* as well as Spielberg's debut, *Duel,* none of which relied heavily on emotion or subtlety to convey their points.

Many would characterize Chris as wooden, and it was true his performance as Collier didn't really seem to flow, but the fault wasn't completely his. With a script that could have used a lot more work, a director who wanted to make the film but didn't seem to understand it, and a costar with whom he seemed to share no chemistry, the deck had been largely stacked against him.

It was unfortunate that it came when it did in his career. Later on he'd have been able to play it better, to have given it more of an edge. Instead, it proved to be a very visible bad move.

But even though it didn't work out, it remained typically adventurous, serving notice that as in everything else, Chris was going to go his own way and not follow the traditionally charted course. Stars didn't do their own stunts; he did. Stars took the part which offered the biggest money; he didn't. It was about much more than getting rich or being a poster on

someone's wall or idolized by millions. Both acting and life—
and in many ways acting *was* life for Chris—were about challenges, always facing something new, always stretching yourself
and learning from the experience. Failure was part and parcel
of that, part of being human, and Chris would learn from that,
too. At twenty-six there were still plenty of years ahead.

And in the meantime, Superman was calling again.

CHAPTER SIX

Somewhere in Time seemed as if it might be something of an interlude in Chris's ongoing Superman saga. Indeed, the entire first decade of his movie career would be dominated by the boots and cape, more than enough to leave him forever indelibly associated with the character.

There was going to be a *Superman II,* the Salkinds insisted. While they'd been forced to abandon their original plan, to shoot both movies simultaneously, because of time and money constraints, the first film had been so globally successful that a sequel was inevitable.

But even as they took their initial steps toward it, they found themselves in the midst of all kinds of legal wranglings. Brando was suing them, as were others; they'd made a mistake in very basic math—offering out more than 100 percent of the film—and been discovered.

Richard Donner wouldn't be returning, and much of the footage he'd shot for the second film was scrapped. Richard Lester, the man who'd been brought in to keep Donner on the straight and narrow with the original, was unsurprisingly named as director in his stead.

To everyone's surprise, for a while it looked as though Chris might not be back. His original contract had stipulated that he'd be paid a quarter of a million dollars to shoot both films together. But, because of problems well out of Chris's control, that hadn't happened. Now the Salkinds wanted him to commit another seven months of his valuable time for no compensation.

That just wasn't going to be acceptable. Chris's agent, who'd been wringing his hands at the money his client had been turning down, went to work on the producers, pointing out that Chris's contract had been allowed to lapse, so if they wanted him—and there was no question that they did, since his appeal had been a big part of *Superman*'s success—they'd better be prepared to pay. And pay quite a bit more than a quarter of a million dollars this time.

When the Salkinds threatened legal action, Chris's lawyers pointed out that he'd been perfectly willing to shoot both films simultaneously. He'd upheld his part of the bargain to the letter and been a perfect gentleman. Even now he was in Japan promoting the first film. What more goodwill and grace could he show?

In the end the Salkinds had no choice but to capitulate; that much had been evident from the first. But they still didn't end up paying a fortune for Chris, even though he'd made one for them. The five-hundred-thousand-dollar fee agreed upon was the same amount he'd made for *Somewhere in Time,* a much smaller film. And it was less than half the sum they were paying Gene Hackman—who also claimed that much-coveted top billing—to reprise his Lex Luthor role.

With the new contracts signed, and preproduction quickly out of the way, work began immediately on *Superman II,* which meant that Chris didn't get any kind of break. From upper Michigan he went directly to the first location shooting for this new epic.

And this time the locations were truly many and varied: from

Niagara Falls to Norway, Paris to St. Lucia. *Superman* had been a blockbuster, and the Salkinds wanted this to be even better; no expense would be spared in the filming, which helped calm the fears Chris had that the Salkinds simply wanted a fast, cheap sequel as a moneymaking machine.

Margot Kidder was back, too, but Lois Lane wasn't going to be as prominent as she had been in the first movie, partly because Kidder had accused the Salkinds of cheating her out of forty thousand dollars. Even though she did eventually receive her money, she paid for it in other ways, although she insisted she didn't care.

"I love Lois Lane," she said, "I could play her till I die, but I'm not going to die if I don't play her."

But *Superman II* was going to be the movie where Lois would finally get her man. Doing that, though, would also prove to be nearly the death of Margot Kidder. Zoran Perisic, who'd created the special effects for the first film, and won an Oscar for his work, had created a new system for the flying effects, much to Chris's pleasure. Instead of the wires and harnesses that chafed and left calluses on his skin, Perisic had made transparent body molds for the actors. They were placed in them on top of forty-foot poles and moved along a series of runners in the studio. It was physically more comfortable, and certainly less demanding than having to keep the body still for ten minutes at a time.

For the most part, this system worked very well, but on one occasion there was a problem.

"I was doing a flight scene with Margot Kidder," Chris recalled, "when the area that was supporting us started to collapse. I ran for her and grabbed her in my arms to stop her from falling. That's what Superman would have done. Obviously, that wouldn't have saved either of us but at that moment exactly, I really believed I was Superman."

And it was perhaps lucky for Kidder that he did. But it was

also a perfectly natural reflex reaction for Chris. Just as in the original, Chris was a very physical presence in *Superman II,* performing all his own stunts, even hanging over Niagara Falls to complete filming on one flying sequence.

Once again, although contractually he shouldn't have been, he was flying and gliding on his own time—not with a cape, but in his plane. He kept it secret, but one incident came close to blowing it all. Gliding in England, a weather change forced him to make a quick landing. He found a three-thousand-yard runway and put down, only to be surrounded by police—not exactly what he'd expected.

"The officers walked over to me and asked, 'Are you aware that you've landed on a secret research center?' I said, 'No, it's not marked on the map.' They replied, 'If we marked it on the map, then it wouldn't be secret, would it?' "

However, this was an instance where fame worked in his favor. After *Superman,* Chris's face was well known, and he wasn't held on spying or trespass charges; the police even allowed him to dismantle his glider and arrange to have it moved.

Challenge of any kind stimulated him, brought him alive, and during a break from the studio filming in Pinewood, in December 1979, Chris found himself facing the biggest challenge of his life—becoming a father. He'd been absent for virtually all of Gae's pregnancy, working on *Somewhere in Time* and now *Superman II.*

As the big moment drew near, he initially decided not to be present for the delivery, but finally there was enough pride and curiosity, and enough of the New Man inside him to overcome the traditionalist and have him present at the birth. It was a decision he didn't regret for a second when Matthew Reeve finally came into the world on December 20 at London's Welbeck Hospital.

"There was a great satisfaction when Matthew came forth and I was the first person he saw. He was placed on Gae's stomach and opened one eye and took a look at me. The first human he saw was me! That was the kind of thrill that is really indescribable, and I think I would really have missed something if I hadn't been there. It strengthens the bond between the three of you tremendously."

However strong the bond was, though, it didn't stop Chris quickly packing his bags and taking off for Switzerland and skiing, hardly the normal action of a new father. When questioned, he pointed out that this was his first break since before *Somewhere in Time,* and that several months more filming were waiting once he returned. He needed the break.

Even Gae, who must have wanted him close by in those first days of parenthood, came to his defense.

"He works so hard," she told *People,* "and besides, afterbirth blues were setting in and I didn't want him to see me weepy."

Whatever the root cause—and it was quite possible that he was simply frightened by the new responsibility of being a parent—the birth, and Chris's sudden departure, led gossips to wonder just what was going on in Chris's relationship with Gae. Was it falling apart? Would they marry? The general consensus seemed to be that marriage was in the cards. After all, they were parents now, so they owed it to themselves and their son to do the sensible, adult thing.

Even the couple themselves didn't seem sure what road they'd take. Chris was bitterly angry when one magazine termed Matthew illegitimate, a harsh term but one that was legally true.

"He's not illegitimate," Chris answered. "His name is Reeve. He calls me Daddy. I was in the delivery room when he was born. I'm with him twenty-four hours a day when I'm not working."

That wasn't, of course, strictly accurate. He'd gone off to Switzerland, and Chris and Gae were in the financial and social position where they could afford to hire a nanny. But his point was made.

Being a mother, Gae, on the other hand, seemed to look at things slightly differently, a little more protective of her family, and with one eye on the future.

"One illegitimate child is fine," she said, "but two is, well, tacky."

It seemed to indicate that if she was going to have more children—and with one barely born, that had to be a large if— she wanted marriage.

Whatever decision the couple was going to come to would have to wait, with Chris off again, completing the filming of *Superman II*. This time the location proved to be far less hospitable than the sun and sand of St. Lucia (where cast and crew had all decamped to film a single scene), with a trip to northern Norway, where an interview Chris gave to a journalist managed to raise the ire of the country's population.

"We're about ten minutes from the North Pole," Chris recounted to Clifford Terry, "way the hell up there, five and a half hours north of Oslo by car. We're staying at this old hotel and having a gay time getting drunk every night and playing billiards and having these incredible meals—wonderful time—and I'm doing this shot. I'm standing out in the middle of the road and there's nothing but mountains and snow and polar bears, and this Norwegian reporter shows up, having tracked the company all the way from Oslo to get a quote from Superman."

The quote he got was that Chris "loved being in the middle of nowhere," and that didn't sit too well with the Norwegians. It was obvious that Chris loved the country, and he was enough of a gentleman never to idly disparage someone's homeland, but they didn't react pleasantly to outsiders referring to their country as a tundra, even when he was talking about an area far removed from any metropolis. Finally the brouhaha reached such proportions that the film company was forced to issue an apology on Chris's behalf, noting that what he "was really saying was that after the hustle and bustle of the big city, how refreshing it is to come to your country, with its peaceful, tranquil solitude." It was fudging, and everybody on both sides knew it, but face was saved and it settled the ruffled feathers. The crew finished their shot and quietly returned to Pinewood.

The experience of filming *Superman II* was much smoother than the original. The money was there, with no worries about it running out this time, there was no directorial conflict, and there was no specter of Brando and his millions of dollars hanging over the whole thing. It had a unified, let's-pull-together feel. But Chris ultimately thought some of the credit should go to ousted director Richard Donner.

"We missed Dick very much, all of us," he said in the *Los Angeles Times.* "Throughout the film we tried to preserve his style and intentions. It was very much as if he were the architect who'd done the blueprint and we were just the contractors."

Architect or no, Donner's name never appeared on the film.

Chris finished all his work on the movie in late spring 1980. It had been a good time, since his dealings had been with Richard Lester, rather than directly with the Salkinds. In fact, everything had been good enough, with a warm enough afterglow, that he was willing to contemplate playing a superhero for the third time.

"No question. I never forget how much I owe Superman. If it hadn't been for him, I wouldn't be talking to you. I'd probably be out there parking cars."

Superman paid the bills, there was no question of that, and paid them quite handsomely. Now that he was more relaxed and comfortable with both the character and the idea of appearing on film, Chris could really appreciate that. Nine months of a cape and tights allowed him a lot of luxuries, like disappearing for the summer to Williamstown, Massachusetts, where he'd performed twelve years before, as a teenager.

He'd been accepted for the two-month summer season at the Williamstown Theatre, committing to work in three plays, *The Cherry Orchard, The Front Page,* and *The Heiress,* and earning the princely sum of $225 a week. Naturally, Gae and Matthew traveled with him, and they set up a temporary home in northeastern Massachusetts, close to the ocean.

Gae still had her business to attend to, so on his days off, Chris was in charge of the baby, a new experience for him, and one he still had to adjust to. On one occasion he took Matthew to the beach, leaving his stroller in the shade while he went snorkeling.

"But when I surfaced, Matthew was no longer in the shade. His poor little face was all red on one side. I thought—fried baby. But luckily, he was fine."

It was a quick, and thankfully relatively pain-free, lesson in child care. From that point on Chris knew he had to take a slightly less cavalier attitude toward looking after his son.

The summer of stage work was like a vacation to him, replenishing his spirit after the long, grueling months of take after take of the same scene. Returning as an adult, he realized that he loved both the Williamstown area and the theater there. They seemed to center him and offer the "breathing space" he needed.

The present was being taken care of with the round of plays and the presence of his family, but like any actor, Chris needed to be looking ahead. *Somewhere in Time* might have bombed with audiences, but that didn't mean Chris's stock had fallen; quite the opposite. Already there was quite a buzz about *Superman II,* that it would be even better than the original, and Chris was seen as one of the hottest leading men around, part of an up-and-coming generation with Harrison Ford, Richard Gere, and John Travolta.

The new opportunities were arriving thick and fast with his agent, and once more Chris was asserting his independence by turning most of them down immediately. Stardom for its own sake, he'd decided, was "just a waste of time."

"If you are a star, you just occupy a special corner of the market and try to be the best product of yourself that you can be, and you stay there. But if you want to act, you have to keep saying, 'All right, I don't know where it's going to take me or what I'm going to do. I'm not going to worry about image.' "

Money, though more than welcome, given that he'd established a fairly luxurious lifestyle and wanted to keep it, was not going to be the yardstick by which he lived his life. That became quite apparent when he refused a massive $1.5 million to star in a film, opting instead for art over commerce.

He'd been offered the lead in Lanford Wilson's new play, *Fifth of July,* a chance to star on Broadway in a drama by one of America's leading playwrights. It was a sequel to *Talley's Folly,* which had won Wilson the Pulitzer Prize. That seemed a far more tantalizing prospect to Chris.

Although he'd be on the Great White Way, Chris's role would be far from glamorous, portraying a bitter, gay, paraplegic Vietnam veteran. He considered it an honor to be asked, especially since the request had come from Wilson himself. It was the type of part any serious actor would almost kill to have, and Chris didn't even have to think twice before answering yes.

The salary was very good by theatrical standards—five thousand dollars a week or 7.5 percent of the gross, whichever sum was larger—but it wasn't about to make him a rich man the way movies could. He was quite literally putting his money where his mouth was.

Fifth of July represented another peak for him, another challenge. The last time he'd appeared on Broadway had been in a supporting role, barely noticed by the critics. This time, back as a star, they couldn't ignore him, and he'd have to win them—and their innate prejudice against "film stars"—over, as well as captivate an audience. Far more than any screen role, it was a supreme test of his acting abilities.

August over, and Chris's time at Williamstown complete, he, Gae, and Matthew moved back to New York, where he began rehearsals.

In a few quarters there was immediate uproar over the choice of Christopher Reeve as Kenneth Talley. Gay activists felt quite strongly that the character, as a gay man, should be portrayed by a gay actor. In fact, once the play had begun its run, three actors from the Gay Activists Alliance confronted Chris backstage before a performance. He asked them to watch him, "and tell me if I had done anything to offend gay pride. They came back after the show and said they had been absolutely devastated by it. The part had worked."

To him, it was all acting, creating the illusion and getting the audience to suspend their disbelief—in other words, using his God-given talent.

"Why should I have a problem playing a homosexual, since the only difference is that the object of my affection is different? Whether you are in love with your car or your stamp collection, the feeling is the same. You don't put a value judgment on it. You don't say, 'Gee, I'm straight.' "

The production teamed him with a number of stalwarts from the New York stage, with people like Swoosie Kurtz and Jeff Daniels (who, despite his abysmal later movie career, was a fine actor) as his support. Still, throughout, the focus was on *him*. He had to carry the play. He had to rely on his years of theatrical experience, far more extensive than most of the public could ever imagine, and his colleagues to see him through every performance.

"*Innocence,*" he said. "Innocence is the key. Innocence means I'm going onstage not knowing any more than I need to know at this moment and I'm going to trust that as we roll along and we get to those big moments, all the homework that I've done, all the life that I've lived, all my trust in the other actors is going to allow something real to happen, where just like in life I don't know how I'm going to respond."

His "homework" for the role had been quite extensive. He was approaching this, as it deserved, with the utmost respect and seriousness. For a week he lived in a VA hospital, spending his days with former soldiers from Vietnam and World War II, some of whom, like Kenneth Talley, were paraplegics.

On top of that, he made several visits to another paraplegic, Mike Sulsona, a man who, like Kenneth Talley, had lost both his legs in Vietnam, and who showed Chris the way a man would walk with arm braces and artificial legs. Unlike Talley, he'd fashioned a positive life for himself.

"He taught me the meaning of optimism," Chris said. "He's lost his legs, but he's become a painter, sculptor, playwright, he's married and has a three-month-old baby. He's become somebody."

He was able to put his lessons to good use, both directly and indirectly. Sulsona's humanity showed in Chris's portrayal of Talley: "His journey in the play is that he finally reaches out and embraces people."

But Chris was also able to make the crowds believe he had no legs. In the script Talley had to fall and Chris "learned to do the stunt so that literally when I fell backward it would get a gasp from the audience because they had believed in the illusion all evening."

Naturally, the name of Christopher Reeve was a big attraction in itself to theatergoers, bringing in plenty of people who'd probably never heard of Lanford Wilson, but wanted to see Superman in more intimate confines. Like it or not, he was a star, and stars sold tickets.

When the play had originally been performed in workshop, it was William Hurt—Chris's old friend and classmate—who'd played Talley. But for Broadway you needed the biggest names to compete, and Hurt (who'd starred in the recently released *Altered States*) was off making the movie that would bring him star status—*Body Heat.*

The cast settled into the New Apollo Theater, completed rehearsals, and were set for the November 5 opening. For Chris it was both a luxury and a novelty to be working and also to be home every night with Gae and Matthew, a very welcome change from months of location shooting.

Everything seemed to be coming together well in the production. But even more than with movies, it seemed to be the critics who ultimately decided the fate of a play in New York. And in the newspapers of November 6, they pronounced judgment.

Frank Rich, in the *New York Times,* thought that Hurt had done a better job as Talley than Chris, who "works earnestly, and in later scenes lets us see some of Kenny's pain. But by then it's too late. His placid face never suggests someone who has lost his legs in the hell of Southeast Asia, and his voice lacks presence and maturity. At most, he gives us the wry surface of the character."

Newsweek's Jack Kroll, one of Chris's big supporters, felt that "Christopher Reeve, whose charming performance in the movie *Superman* was underrated, is a young but long-committed stage actor, and he's effective and winning."

Time, on the other hand, took a completely different stance, remarking glibly that "through the miracle of commercial casting, cinema's Superman has become a homosexual cripple. Reeve gives the role his old college try—fervent amateurism."

Meanwhile, *Women's Wear Daily,* in the person of Howard Kissel, might almost have been seeing something completely different, as he wrote that Chris "gives a sensitive performance, punctuated by a scathing wit. Reeve makes it a deeply believable part of the character rather than just a way of getting laughs." The critics were obviously strongly divided. Amazingly, though, that didn't seem to hurt attendance figures. Whether because of Chris's presence in the cast, or the fact that this was a major new play by a Pulitzer Prize winner on Broadway, it was a hit.

Chris readily admitted that on the opening night he'd been "wooden," but also felt that he'd been unfairly judged—as a movie star taking a dilettante turn, rather than as an actor.

Once he'd fully settled into the part, he claimed he was pleased with his performance, calling it "the thing I'm proudest of in my career so far."

He had been Kenneth Talley for little more than a month when *Superman II* opened all over the world—everywhere except America. In South Africa the film immediately set box-office records.

A Superman movie not opening in America? What was going on?

It seemed a backward way of working, even downright ridiculous, to have an American film open abroad first—it would be the middle of 1981 before American audiences would be able to see it—but there was a method to what seemed liked madness.

Superman had done particularly well in what were now being termed the "international markets"—it was one of the first films to alert Hollywood to how lucrative they could be. So this was an experiment of sorts, a gamble, but one that ended up paying off quite handsomely, bringing millions of dollars into the Hollywood coffers, and sending anticipation for the American release soaring through the roof.

Chris was obviously happy with his work in the movie, happy enough to get a print and screen it for the cast of *Fifth of July,* who were real fellow professionals, and a tough audience to please.

It was, he asserted to a reporter, "much better than part one. It's not so heavy, it's not so pretentious. This one has a much lighter tone and there's much more action and humor. I mean, it got a standing ovation [from the *Fifth of July* cast] at the end. I think people are going to like it."

Chris stayed with *Fifth of July* for almost five months, leaving the cast in March of 1981. He'd thoroughly enjoyed his time there, the communal feeling of the production—which would eventually be nominated for five Tony Awards, with Swoosie Kurtz being named Best Actress—and, most particularly, being home by 11:30 every night. He was relaxed and happy, even appearing on Merv Griffin's talk show and playing piano, demonstrating a side of himself that most people didn't know existed.

But, as he had all his life, he felt the need for new challenges, new areas to push. He'd conquered Kenneth Talley; that was done. Greener pastures were waiting for him—in particular a new movie, which would have him costarring with another of the film greats, Michael Caine.

CHAPTER SEVEN

It was only March, and 1981 was already shaping up to be Chris's busiest year as a professional actor. He'd been replaced onstage by Richard Thomas (better known to millions as John-Boy Walton) in *Fifth of July*. He was set to begin filming *Deathtrap*, with Michael Caine. As soon as the shooting of that was complete, there would be all the publicity for the American release of *Superman II*, and then he planned to return to Williamstown to take part in their summer season.

That should have been plenty to keep anybody occupied, but just to make sure he'd stay busy he'd also developed a commercial venture, "a publicity stunt," as he called it, named Reeve Air. Essentially it was a charter service to help defray the expenses of the Beech Baron he kept parked at Teterboro Airport in New Jersey. His name lent cachet, although it was the pilots at Beech East who got the flying work (Chris couldn't be one of his own pilots, since he didn't have a commercial license). Businessmen and others were actually chartering Chris's airplane, and he received a commission on each deal. It wasn't a big business, not really registered, but it helped pay for one of his hobbies.

★ ★ ★

xcellent as he was, Michael Caine wasn't the sole reason Chris
had taken the part in *Deathtrap*. The script, by Jay Presson Allen,
from Ira Levin's play, was taut, and it would also give him the
chance to work with Sidney Lumet, one of the "varsity" he'd
referred to in awe a couple of years before.

As in *Fifth of July*, Chris was playing a gay man, which, he
hoped, would certainly get him away from any Superman stereo-
typing. He needed to try and establish himself as a versatile
actor to the moviegoing public, and the best way, he thought,
was to take parts as far removed from a hero as he could find.

"I wouldn't take a part unless it was weird," he admitted later.
"I had a little weirdness period. . . . If you give me a script,
I've got to be either psychotic, homosexual, or in some other
strange way corrupt." It was a reaction, of course, but a perfectly understandable one.

What he didn't know, although he'd find out when shooting began, was that ironically it was the Man of Steel who'd
got him the part. As Lumet told him when they met on the
set, "Anyone who can make me believe they're Superman can
be in my movie."

Before that meeting, though, he had some real work to do
researching the role. Like most serious actors, research and more
research was the foundation of his characterizations. It gave
him a grounding on which he could build all of his ideas. And
to be a murderous psychotic, what better than to spend the
final daylight hours of his Broadway run with criminal psy-
chologists at Bellevue Medical Center?

Given that *Deathtrap* had been a stage play, the filming was
relatively straightforward. For once, Chris wasn't traveling hither
and yon to locations, but was spending his time purely on a
soundstage. To his delight, Lumet chose to treat it like a play,
scheduling daily rehearsals in the mornings for the cast. For
Chris, this was well-trodden turf. Michael Caine, however, wasn't

as happy with the exercise. He didn't have Chris's stage background, his long career having been purely in movies. But, albeit reluctantly, because he was a true professional, he did what was asked of him, and a chemistry developed between Caine and Chris, which was necessary given the ongoing gay theme of the plot, right down to the kiss the two shared in one scene.

In fact, Chris joked, "Michael and I had a real *La Cage Aux Folles* routine going off-camera to get in the mood."

It was an intimate film, and the setting Lumet chose made it seem more confined, even deliberately claustrophobic. It was never intended to be the type of work that would bring in record grosses—Middle America simply didn't want to see gay murder mysteries—but with a modest budget of $10.5 million, it didn't need to do *that* well to cover its costs, and Michael Caine and Chris would bring in audiences on their names alone.

But Chris didn't have the time to sit around and consider the film's prospects. No sooner was filming done than *Superman II* was finally due to be released in America, and there was the usual welter of publicity, benefits, and premieres that he had to attend, the biggest being a prescreening brunch with Vice President George Bush.

It was, perhaps, appropriate, as Superman saved America (and the world) in this film, topping it all off by replacing the dome on the White House. And the new Reagan administration was eager to embrace the sort of basic "truth, justice, and the American way" apple pie values that Superman personified.

Notably, the final credits of the movie announced that *Superman III* would be coming soon. Chris had already said he was willing to reprise his role, but beyond that, the Salkinds were being more hopeful than anything. Outside America, *Superman II* had done well, but hadn't quite been the blockbuster the first had been. The gamble of opening it outside the borders of the red, white, and blue hadn't paid off in the way they'd hoped. What they needed in the United States was good reviews and marvelous numbers.

The reviews, at least, were everything they could have hoped for. In the *New York Times,* Vincent Canby seemed to encapsulate the critics' feelings when he wrote, "It's that rare film phenomenon—a movie far better than the one that prompted it."

The *Los Angeles Times* pointed out, quite rightly, that "the film's fun comes from the character, dialogue, and performance, not effects . . . [although] there are, of course, enough effects to fill a dozen Saturday matinee serials."

Really, *Superman II* offered more scope than its predecessor. The story of Kal-El, the boy sent from Krypton, had already been told (although it was rehashed over what might have been the longest opening credits in movie history). This could concentrate on Superman, and it certainly did.

One of the riders Chris had included in his contract was that Superman be portrayed without pomposity and with humor. And through most of the film that would be done—all the way to his sensitive side once Lois Lane discovered his secret identity.

Chris really did have to act in this—there was far more to his character than action scenes and a dimpled smile here. In its serious moments—directed with the kind of touch that would have elevated *Somewhere in Time* above the mundane—he was able to use minimal gestures to portray complex emotions. Comparing it to the original, it was obvious that Chris had come a long way in a very short time as an actor. He'd learned his craft over a number of years on the stage, but becoming a star had forced him to improve by leaps and bounds, even if it hadn't always been apparent on-screen. The callow lead of *Somewhere in Time* had turned into a real presence.

Certainly the reviewers enjoyed his work, finding plenty to praise in his acting. Sheila Benson singled out the moment

Clark Kent admitted his dual life to Lois Lane, "directed like an old vaudeville turn, a change of character with the actor's back to you. When Clark Kent finally drops all pretenses and turns around to face Lois as Superman, with no intervening phone booth, the moment pays off perfectly."

In *New York,* David Denby had to single him out from a cast filled with fine actors by noting that "good as they are, the comic-heroic mixture wouldn't jell without Christopher Reeve's sweet, courtly presence at its center. . . . Reeve's bashful gallantry is thoroughly winning. . . . [His] little smile and charming modesty make the conceit work."

He'd delivered the film performance he was truly capable of, and it was paying off well. Certainly the initial numbers were impressive. In its first week, *Superman II* took in $24 million, a new American record, and although the dollars dipped somewhat (in the end, it didn't take in as much as the original), the general consensus was that this was the better film.

Warners even tried to get Chris an Oscar nomination for his work, something he never expected, and believed was futile.

"When Warner Brothers told me . . . I said, 'Save your bucks. Spend them on someone else. It's hopeless.' "

And it was. Chris was portrayed in the press as being angry and upset when he wasn't nominated, but Superman wasn't the kind of role that was likely to bring anyone an Academy Award (Best Actor in 1980 went to Robert De Niro, for *Raging Bull*—*Superman II* had enjoyed a couple of American screenings in December 1980 to qualify for that year's Oscars), and he was enough of a realist to understand that. It was entertainment, and not art, and thus seen as something slightly inferior, although he did add, in an interview with Gene Siskel, that "it would be nice if performances could be judged on merit alone and without regard to the kind of film they're in, so that it would be acceptable if you give a good performance in what turns out to be a big box-office film."

Gratifying as awards and nominations might be, Chris was focused enough not to lose sight of the fact that he was an actor because he loved acting. Becoming a star was little more than a lucky break, and he knew it. But at whatever level, he'd still be involved in the theater, and that was where he was going to return, to Williamstown for July and August, and a small role in *The Greeks,* in its American premiere.

The play itself, which had originally been performed in 1980 by the Royal Shakespeare Company, lasted a grueling five hours. Adapted from Euripides, it ambitiously told the story of the Trojan War and the House of Atreus.

Although a big household name by now, in Williamstown Chris was just another member of the company, which reunited him with Celeste Holm, in whose play he'd toured directly after high school, as well as introducing him to talents like Edward Herrmann and Blythe Danner (whose daughter, Gwyneth Paltrow, was also in the cast).

Williamstown represented a chance to escape from the increasing pressures of life as a star. With Gae and Matthew in tow, "I wander around the town barefoot, and nobody bothers me. Those of us who are 'names' get enough attention elsewhere."

Simply, he was glad to be involved in any way with the Williamstown Theatre. The place, the people, the area, held a magic for him, and the productions kept him on his toes. *The Greeks,* with its classical subject matter, held particular appeal.

"Nikos [Psacharopoulos, artistic director] sent me the script, but I told him I'd do it without even reading the script. I said, 'Nikos, tell me what to do and I'll do it.' This is the first classical part I've played since I was a drama student at Juilliard in

1974. You can't come on like a plumber. For me, Williamstown is like a continuing adult-education program."

The success of *Superman II* made Chris into even more of a public figure than he'd been before, which meant that once again his private life came under the scrutiny of the press. Never mind that he was a father, happily settled into a relationship. The fact remained that he and Gae weren't married, and that meant the gossips could have a field day.

Invariably, whenever he was seen in the company of some other woman—and when he was away from home he didn't spend every night alone in his hotel room; he had friends and colleagues of both sexes around the world—there was speculation that cracks were appearing between Chris and Gae. He was adamant that that simply wasn't true.

"Before I met Gae, there was a period of hyperactivity," he admitted readily. "I got around at lightning speed, put in a lot of miles. But when I met her, I made a choice and it worked. When you have something good at home, you don't stray."

On location, he did go out for a meal or a drink with other women, all kinds of people whose company he liked. But he always informed Gae; there were no secrets between them. They loved and trusted each other, just like any married couple. The only difference was the ring and the license, but America, taking a rapid political turn to the right, was becoming more conservative almost on a daily basis. If they aren't married, the idea went, they can't really be committed to each other. And in the end, there was no point in denying it. Chris and Gae were merely wasting their breath; people were going to believe what they wanted to believe.

An obviously hurt Chris expressed his feelings to *Parade:* "I've been terribly vulnerable—talking about my child, my relationship with Gae, why we're not married. . . . I've worn my heart on my sleeve. Well, I'm through with that. I don't want to share intimate details. There's nothing in it for me. I'm keeping my personal life closed and my wittily self-deprecating anecdotes for my family and friends. It's not for public consumption anymore."

Who could blame him for feeling so defensive? Although he was a star—like it or not—his private life had come under the microscope with ridiculous speculation that often seemed to have no basis in fact. If they wanted to criticize him as an actor, that was one thing (although he noted in the same interview that he'd stopped reading reviews of his films); it was aimed at the work he exhibited before the public, and thus fair game. But Gae and Matthew were not part of his acting life. What happened away from the camera had nothing to do with the rest of America. Whether he and Gae chose to live together, or marry and renew their vows every year was nobody's business but theirs.

The summer in Williamstown at least gave the three of them time to be together, out of the public eye. Chris was in need of some relaxation after the intense shoot of *Deathtrap,* and his relatively small part in *The Greeks* didn't demand too much, while offering him a great deal of satisfaction. The movies brought him the money to finance times like these, when he made next to nothing but did the work that was really in his heart. It was a trade-off, a compromise, but worthwhile. Without movies, he'd never have had Gae or Matthew, not to mention all the material luxuries in his life. He would, perhaps, still have been coming to Williamstown, but it would have seemed less like a vacation and more like another job.

The two months in Massachusetts were really nothing more than a chance to recharge his batteries, though, a reprieve between film roles. By now his agent knew he wasn't going to take anything obvious. He'd already turned down more plums than most actors were offered in an entire career. To his credit, his choices were artistic. But for his next part he'd signed to play a role even further away from Superman than his *Death-trap* character: Christopher Reeve was going to be a priest, in a film called *Monsignor.*

With the Williamstown season over, Chris, Gae, and Matthew returned to New York, and Chris set about research-ing his role by going to a Catholic retreat in Oak Ridge, New Jersey. For someone who was an admitted "lapsed Episcopalian," it was a strange and slightly disorienting experience at first, but one that he was able to translate into his own life, as any actor needs to be able to do.

"At first I felt very out of place among all these people who had made a real strong choice about their commitment," he admitted in the *New York Post.* "But look, I've been a pro-fessional actor since I was fifteen. Each day is a passport to a new world, so every day requires a new commitment."

By October he was ready to leave for filming in Rome. While most movie stars would have been perfectly content with the pampering of a first-class airline seat, Chris saw this as another opportunity to fly, and to do something he'd never attempted before—cross the Atlantic alone.

The Beech Baron was capable of the journey, but was Chris up to it? He'd flown around America any number of times, but this, as he wanted, would be a real test of his piloting skills. It was a trip he decided to keep from the film's producers, since he "didn't want the studio getting in a flap," as they certainly would have done, knowing their leading man was attempting something so dangerous.

But he just loved to fly; it had reached the point where his contracts now specified that he couldn't go up in his own plane for the duration of shooting.

His attempts to keep his journey quiet, though, soon van-ished in a flight that proved to be far from smooth. He'd planned on refueling in Reykjavík, Iceland, but the information he received from air traffic controllers in Greenland meant he was off course, and likely to run out of fuel over the icy North Atlantic.

"I was one worried fellow for half an hour," he recollected. "Then I decided they had to be wrong. And they were—I landed in Reykjavík five minutes ahead of schedule."

Far from taking that as an omen, giving up, and jumping on a commercial airliner, it spurred him on. He wasn't going to let an ocean defeat him. But luck was against him; the second leg went almost as badly as the first. *Variety* reported that he got lost, and instead of flying into Glasgow airport in Scotland, he ended up some three hundred miles south, at Luton airport, outside London.

Inevitably, the story made all the papers and the producers discovered that Chris still preferred challenge to comfort. It didn't make an auspicious beginning to the two months of autumn filming in Rome, and for Chris things would only get worse, as the tabloids began floating rumors that he and Ursula Andress, one of the great screen sex kittens, were in the middle of a torrid Italian affair, all the more interesting as she wasn't even part of the *Monsignor* cast. While he admitted he had spent some time with Andress, fifteen years his senior, and recently a mother herself, he strenuously denied any romantic involvement. Notably, the leaks about their supposed affair all came from the usual unnamed "inside sources" or anonymous people who'd claimed to have seen them together, hardly the most credible evidence in the world, and yet another reason for Chris to keep his private life resolutely closed and private.

Monsignor, from Jack Alain Leger's book, was hardly guaranteed to win over America's large Catholic audience with its tale of an evil priest who befriended mobsters and seduced a nun. In theory it should have been an interesting role for Chris, one that allowed him to expand on the dark side he'd shown in *Deathtrap.*

Reality proved to be different.

"I played a corrupt priest, not a real priest," he explained later. "What happened in that movie is that they tried to homogenize him, they flattened him out."

But even as Chris was realizing this was becoming a dreadful mistake—which became even more apparent when the sparks between him and Genevieve Bujold, playing the seduced nun, failed to fly—the producers were praising him to the skies.

"Chris is totally believable in the role. There's no way to connect him with the actor who plays Superman."

And that, Chris hoped, was true, but not for the same reasons the producers hoped. Superman was proving to be his bread and butter, the ongoing paycheck that allowed him to do everything else.

As filming progressed, Chris realized more and more that he should never have taken the part. What had seemed like a good idea at the time was proving to be an unmitigated disaster. Awful as it might be, and it would have to await release in 1982 to see just *how* bad that was, it did serve one purpose for Chris.

"It was a necessary failure because it brought me back to my senses and brought me back to me."

By now Chris had to be questioning some of the choices he'd made. He didn't read his reviews anymore, but he knew full well that *Somewhere in Time* had been widely panned, and he could already guess that *Monsignor* would receive an even worse reception. He didn't seem to be picking movies that played to his strengths for his starring roles, but away from them. As Superman he'd been a perfect fit, but beyond that, as a star, he seemed to be foundering.

Deathtrap was something different altogether. He had a leading role, but one which had him playing strongly off another equally powerful character, rather than the reliance being on him alone. Could it be that his best work outside Superman came when he was part of an ensemble, rather than having to carry the production himself? That, after all, was what he was used to in the theater, and it was a feeling he enjoyed. And that prompted another question—was Chris really movie star material? He was a good actor, that much was beyond doubt, and he undeniably had the looks, but was he *really* a star?

Had his Superman role been a fluke, one of those pieces of perfect casting he'd never be able to duplicate? Certainly, to most people he wasn't able to get beyond it. To them Superman was Christopher Reeve and Christopher Reeve was Superman. His other starring roles were Superman in another part, a change of costume, however wildly different they might be.

What he needed was to rethink everything, his whole approach to movies, and the type of parts he was seeking, if he was going to be genuinely happy working in the cinema.

That was what he *needed*. What he got was slightly different. It was a return to prison, in a way—an offer he simply couldn't refuse—to play Superman again.

CHAPTER EIGHT

Two million dollars and top billing to take a role he was already associated with was an impossible offer to walk away from. It offered a good measure of security, both financial and emotional. It was, essentially, a return to the basics that had made him.

The problem, of course, was that Chris hadn't yet managed to establish himself properly as a film actor, and the more he continued to return to Superman, the more it was going to keep dogging him throughout his career; the stronger the association, the more difficult it would be to break, no matter how good his other work might be.

The Salkinds, producing yet again, didn't seem to realize quite what a property they had in Chris, either. He'd carried the first two films, and his face and physique had reestablished Superman in the American psyche as someone of the modern age, but essentially they continued to try and treat him as a nobody, the young man they'd thrust into the limelight. Two million dollars was a handsome paycheck, but it still paled when compared to the amount they were paying Richard Pryor to be the villain—$4 million.

"He's been around longer than I have, and he deserves [it],"

Chris said with remarkable grace. However, that grace no longer extended to the Salkinds, and, like Margot Kidder (who would find herself with barely a line in *Superman III*), he called them "untrustworthy, devious, and unfortunate people," harsh words from a man who was generally remarkably temperate with his tongue in public.

There would be no return for Gene Hackman, nor for Ned Beatty or Valerie Perrine—their parts had been little more than cameos in the second film, anyway. Instead the producers offered up Robert Vaughan *(The Man from U.N.C.L.E.),* jazz singer Annie Ross, and Pamela Stephenson, while Annette O'Toole was brought in as Superman's new love interest, Lana Lang.

But as preproduction was taking place, Chris had other things on his mind—the opening of *Deathtrap*. Even if he didn't bother to read his notices anymore, he must have known in his gut that this was a deliciously good movie, and he'd done some outstanding work in it.

He even took his father to a private screening, something he'd never done before. Franklin Reeve wasn't exactly a maven of popular culture, but Chris believed he'd enjoy this, with its sly twists and turns and humor.

Chris, as playwright Clifford Anderson, had a perfect working partner in Michael Caine. Even taking place mostly on a small set—a house in East Hampton, New York—it managed the intimacy of a stage play without its claustrophobia, a tribute to Sidney Lumet's light direction. Its crosses, double crosses, and triple crosses kept heightening the tension, running the gamut from camp to serious to hilarious, all the way to the O. Henry jolt at the end. With subtle little flourishes to his body language and speech, Chris emphasized Cliff's effeminate side without ever falling into a mincing stereotype.

For the first time on film, Chris had the chance to really

stretch himself, and show the breadth of his talent, and why he'd become such a strong stage actor. And whether he read their words or not, the critics had plenty of praise for his work in the film.

"These two actors tread a fine line between being captivatingly theatrical and simply being a pair of hambones," Gene Siskel wrote in the *Chicago Tribune*. "If I had to choose one performance over another, I would choose Reeve's, simply because he is so good at getting intensely angry without seeming silly."

And the *Washington Post* suggested that "he ingratiates himself in a fresh way by impersonating a charming menace, extending his range to the amoral, treacherous aspects of human nature."

Still, as *People* noted, "Reeve does the desired damage to his Superman image by kissing Caine full on the mouth," hardly the point of it all, but one of many twists. Even with that little shock, they couldn't quite recommend the movie.

Finally, it seemed, Chris was living up to the potential that had been bubbling under the celluloid surface for four years now. If one movie seemed to offer him the chance to establish an identity away from Superman and show a strong actor's personality of his own, this was it.

The only problem was that not many people saw it. However good its notices, the public in the early 1980s wanted big entertainment, big names in big roles with big budgets, and preferably big special effects. *Deathtrap* had the names, but that was all. It was, by design, a small film, but a little gem hidden among the blockbusters. In its quest to be overawed, America missed a treat, although the film did manage to end up in the black.

Chris claimed to be happy just doing the best work he could.

"I really thought I'd act in regional theaters for the rest of my life," he said. "I never expected stardom. So I'm not complaining."

However, he wasn't able to capitalize on this new base once *Monsignor* was released. From a zenith he moved straight to a nadir.

It was an artistic and commercial disaster. Even a naked Genevieve Bujold could barely make it limp past its opening weekend.

In *Newsweek,* Jack Kroll wrote that "only his best friend or his best accountant can explain why the talented Reeve signed on for this ecclesiastical geek of a movie, which wins the 'Inchon' award as the most gangrenous Turkey of the Month."

And that was one of the kinder reviews. It really was so badly done that what should have been drama came across like bad comedy, causing the *Los Angeles Times* to muse that "as guided by [director] Frank Perry, Reeve is not only at sea in any of these emotions, his performance is somehow familiar. . . . When his postulant-lover, Genevieve Bujold, presses him to reveal his troubling secret, [you expect] what he will blurt out is not, 'I'm a *priest,*' but 'I can fly!' "

In the movie business, one bomb, even two, is far from a career-ending proposition. Perry was coming off a big hit *(Mommie Dearest),* but this was so bad that it would be three years after *Monsignor* before another of his films made it to the screen.

Not surprisingly, there was a big Catholic backlash against *Monsignor,* not only in America, but all over the world. The Church was an institution not to be treated badly, even by the mighty Hollywood. Chris was lucky to escape the wrath, but by then he'd already suffered enough at the pens of the critics.

What perhaps made it worse was the fact that every word was justified. Everyone involved would have been done a great favor if all the prints had been burned before the public had a chance to see them.

In his three roles away from Superman, Chris had proved himself to be extremely erratic, going from bad to excellent to just plain awful. Part of the blame (or credit) had to go to the directors, but a lot had to be assumed by Chris himself. When it came to the crunch, so far he hadn't been able to draw consistently good performances out of himself. He was a star by virtue of Superman. To be able to break away from that and achieve renown as a movie *actor*, he would need to pull several stunning roles in a row out of his hat.

At the same time, no one was about to dismiss him out of hand. In his own quiet way, he'd built up a lot of goodwill, both within the industry and with the public. His acting choices so far hadn't always been the best, but at least he'd approached them honestly and earnestly, always eager to give it all, and people appreciated that. In interviews he came across as thoughtful, articulate, and dignified beyond his years, far from overawed by his own stature. He was the type of star that America, and indeed the world, loved to love, another James Stewart or even Henry Fonda. The tabloids seemed to enjoy dredging up rumor and gossip about his private life, but the fact was that he remained a committed family man, a strong partner and father. He saw one of his responsibilities as keeping Gae and Matthew as far away from the spotlight as he could, and shielded them.

Gae wasn't, and never would be, a typical "movie wife," content to hang on her husband's arm. They were seen together, at parties, premieres, discos, but she'd continued to build her business, and become quite successful in her own right. When Chris received his $2 million paycheck for *Superman III,* he invested some of it in her modeling agency, Legends, feeling that he'd end up making money.

She was every bit as international as Chris, shuttling with Matthew and his nanny between her offices in New York and London, and still maintaining homes in both cities.

Matthew saw his father less than most sons; filmmaking was hardly a typical nine-to-five job. But then again, Chris wasn't a typical dad. How many fathers could take a three-year-old flying in their own plane, or gliding, skiing, or sailing? And in the time he wasn't working, Chris was able to share these things with his son, to give him constant attention and have the kind of relationship and closeness he'd never had with his own father.

The pain of his parents' divorce had never left Chris, and he certainly didn't want his own kid to have to go through something similar. There was a lot he could offer Matthew, not just financially, but also emotionally, a stability, a bonding, that he desperately wanted to be able to give.

"The key to being a good father is never to think you own your child—you don't. Why, Matthew's a real person. He's just short!"

Once again, though, in 1982, he had to be away from home for an extended period, as the filming for *Superman III* began. This time around, Chris wanted to give more depth to Clark Kent. He'd already achieved the lightness; now it was time to have a little more heft and avoid the possibility of caricature.

"I tried to give Clark Kent a new dimension," he told Guy Delcourt, "to show his gentility, his need to do good, his friendliness, instead of continuing to portray him as a comic personality or as a slapstick character."

He also offered his opinion as to why there was no love story in the new film. It was, he explained, something he respected, because Superman had fallen in love "once and for all in *Superman II*." Superman had slept with Lois and then erased her memory of the affair. "He does this because he feels that he can handle the pain of their separation more easily than she can."

But it was also a fact that there was absolutely no chemistry between Chris and Annette O'Toole's Lana Lang. What romance occurred would be described by O'Toole as "bittersweet, not hot and heavy," which was almost a metaphor for the entire film.

Somewhere along the line, the film's basic idea of going deeper into Superman, and revealing more about him, had been lost in the rewrites. Even five weeks spent filming in Alberta—substituting for the American Midwest on film—didn't seem to illuminate much of anything.

The Salkinds had a budget, and they planned on using it, all $35 million of it. The theory, which would become prevalent in Hollywood, was that if you spent and spent to overwhelm an audience, they'd be happy. And so locations and effects were piled heavily upon each other, as if they could substitute for a plot.

The first two films in the series had managed to enhance the Superman legend. But, more than anything else, their popularity had been due to Chris's courtly performance as the Man of Steel. The action scenes were state-of-the-art for their time, but it was the image of Chris in cape and boots that remained in the public's memory, seeing everything with a gentle, compassionate (super)humanity. There was drama and comedy in good proportions, enough to offer gentle nudges and winks to the audience, without ever becoming a parody of itself.

During the filming it became apparent that restraint wasn't going to be one of the watchwords on this production. Richard Pryor had been recruited not to play a part, it seemed, but to be Richard Pryor, one of the hottest comedy talents of the period, in a Superman movie. It was as if the Salkinds (with director Richard Lester equally guilty) had sold out the franchise for a quick profit. The quality control that made the first two movies such a delight had vanished entirely. They'd forgotten that the law of diminishing returns didn't necessarily have to set in so quickly—the James Bond films have remained a viable, entertaining series for many years—as long as a certain amount of care was exercised.

For Chris, becoming more and more horrified as the shoot dragged on, it was a case of give it his best, get it over with, and get out, back to Gae and Matthew in New York, to try and erase the experience from his mind—only there was no superkiss that could do that.

He came away with even less love for the Salkinds than he'd had going into the filming. Their motive, he said, was no more than "greed," and he continued, "There are some things about commercial filmmaking that are in *really* bad taste. For a film to be commercial, it must earn money, and that results in strategic planning in certain degrees—the goal to earn even *more* money. When it comes down to a showdown between quality and integrity and commercial expedience, guess who wins?"

The answer was going to be self-evident. He'd come away from the whole experience with a very bad taste in his mouth. And even if it had made him a relatively rich man, he wasn't planning on returning.

"Look, I've flown, become evil, loved, stopped and turned the world backward. I've faced my peers, rescued cats from trees. What is there left for Superman to do that hasn't already been done?"

It was a valid question, but it was also one the comic-book writers had been forced to ask themselves for years before coming up with creative solutions. The scriptwriters of *Superman III* had seemed to settle for the lowest common denominator, a fact that wasn't lost on fans.

Also, Chris believed it was time to leave Superman behind, once and for all. The character had given him so much, there could be no doubt of that—in each of his homes, in his plane or glider, he saw the results—but its time had passed. Before it became too late, he was determined to establish himself as a film *actor*, rather than a star.

"I decided back in 1981, when I read the script for *Superman III*. I said, 'I'll do it,' because I'd said I'd do it, but it wasn't up to the mark. Something was missing. They left out the warmth and the humor."

What he needed and craved were roles with the depth and complexity of his part in *Deathtrap*. Nothing flashy, but something to challenge him, to give him a chance to properly parade his art.

"I wanted to be an actor, not run around with a machine gun," was the way he characterized it to *Entertainment Weekly*.

His agent came up with two possibilities. The first was a remake of *Mutiny on the Bounty*, titled simply *The Bounty*, which would have put him up against Anthony Hopkins, still several years away from his Oscar, but a fine actor nonetheless. Chris would have had the lead in a big-budget production.

"It was tempting," he admitted. "It had a fine Robert Bolt screenplay, Anthony Hopkins, and eighteen weeks in Tahiti but . . . it wasn't for me. I need to get excited and I just couldn't feel it."

The other was far more modest, one of the leads in a Merchant-Ivory production of Henry James's *The Bostonians*.

The choice for a movie star should have been obvious. *The Bounty* was offering $1 million for his services. Merchant-Ivory couldn't manage more than a fraction of that. But Chris was determined to try and live by his words that "I just hope it's a decent piece of work." In spite of the difference in money, he chose *The Bostonians*.

The decision wasn't popular with his agent, to the extent that they quickly ended up parting ways. Nor was it well received by Merchant-Ivory's investors, who didn't believe Chris had what it took to act in a period drama. James Ivory and Ismail Merchant, whose reputations for quality films preceded them, fought hard to keep him, and finally succeeded. They knew whom they wanted, and had ample faith in his ability, even when he was going to be paired with Britain's leading actress, Vanessa Redgrave. They felt him capable of holding his own.

For Chris, this was like a dream come true. Working as part of an ensemble with names like Redgrave, Wallace Shawn, and Linda Hunt was true acceptance by his peers. He hadn't named Merchant-Ivory as part of his dream "varsity" a few years before, but that was merely an oversight. He knew and admired their work, and he was determined to justify their faith in him.

Nineteen eighty-three was rapidly turning into even more of a banner year than 1981, and one where he'd be working just as hard. It was a time of good news. Not only was he doing exactly what he wanted, but he and Gae found out that she was expecting another child, due in December. Ridiculous as it was, once the news got out, they were forced to issue a press release through Chris's secretary that they still weren't planning to marry.

The filming of *Superman III* had occupied Chris for much of 1982, forcing him to abandon plans to spend July and August in Williamstown, but this year the schedules would fall into place, allowing him to act there, as a member of the cast of *Holiday,* headed up by Blythe Danner, and to enjoy two months of peace in the country.

He was even going to film his second television special, this one on a subject close to his heart—celebrity daredevils. Since he loved risk himself, never shying away from it or the opportunity to perform his own stunts, he'd been a natural as host for the ABC special. The year before, the man who'd fought for truth, justice, and the American way had been an obvious participant in *I Love Liberty,* a sentimental look at America and its ideals, perfect for the early Reagan years, and in 1981 he'd guested on *The Muppet Show,* the kind of part any parent of a young child would beg for.

Entertaining as it could be, though, television still remained a second-class medium in his mind. His stepfather had treated it that way when Chris was young, and those childish attitudes, once formed, can prove hard to break. Even playing Prince Charming in Shelly Duvall's *Faerie Tale Theater* adaptation of "Cinderella" for Showtime didn't really change that mindset. It was a fun, small part, but nothing more.

He was geared up to begin work on the spring shoot of *The Bostonians.* The filming took place on Martha's Vineyard, where Chris's brother Ben now lived. Chris already knew the area quite well, having sailed there often with Franklin when he was young, and it was a place where Chris could take his own boat out when he wasn't required on the set. Gae was looking more pregnant by the week, and along with Matthew, by now an inquisitive three-year-old, Chris settled into a rented house at the Vineyard.

The area had long been a favorite summer retreat with the elite of the Northeast, and once people like James Taylor and Carly Simon began moving there in the early seventies, it had even acquired a thin, hip gloss over its old money.

Chris, of course, had always been careful to research his characters, a trait that separated him from many movie stars. Given that this role was especially important for him, something of a last chance to prove he could really do something away from Superman, he was particularly meticulous, reading in depth about Henry James to discover what made the author of *The Bostonians* tick, listening to speech patterns of southerners to first distinguish the accents and then find the one he needed for his character, Basil Ransom.

"I found Basil a very appealing part," he said. "He's part hero, part villain—there's a strong contemporary theme. And with

Merchant-Ivory's reputation for integrity, I knew they would be faithful to Henry James."

In fact, he planned on putting a lot of Clark Gable into his performance, right down to the mustache.

"I think that Clark Gable, wherever he is, would have approved of the way Basil goes about handling his women. The attitude is, well, you can come with me now or you can come with me later, but there's no doubt about it, she's coming with me. If that's done in the right kind of underplayed, gentle, compassionate way, it can work well in a film."

As the filming began, he found his admiration for James Ivory growing and growing. Without a doubt, this was the best film experience he'd ever had.

"What Jim does beautifully," Chris explained, "is to collect people around him who are passionate in their work, and to use the best of what they can do, whether it's the cameraman, the actors, or the costume designers. He absorbs it all, and when he's got all their inputs, he just stands back and uses the best of it. The actors need somebody with a rational and dispassionate intelligence to say, 'Thank you so much for all these things you're bringing me; now here are the ones I want to use.' He's a terrific judge of what's good and what isn't. Sometimes he doesn't know exactly how something should be done better, or what's wrong with it. But he can certainly say, 'No, not that. Let's try something else.' You end up really wanting to please."

And Chris had a great desire to please. He could tell that Ivory was drawing something special from him, the best performance he'd given on film, something genuinely outstanding. How Ivory could do what others hadn't managed intrigued him. What made the difference between the mundane and the extraordinary? The thought planted a small seed, an idea slowly forming at the back of his mind, of eventually directing himself. It was a natural step for an actor, in many ways, to go from playing one part to overseeing others playing many parts, to stamp his own vision on a play, and to make the actors give their best.

For the moment, though, it was little more than a glimmer to tuck away for the future, a spark. There was plenty to relish in working opposite Vanessa Redgrave, a woman whose acting talent transcended any politics.

She had a way with her characters to bring out the best in anyone acting with her—a common quality of all the greats—which Chris certainly appreciated. Grounded as he was in stage work (and movie work by now), and having appeared with a number of major names, this was still an education for him.

Perhaps surprisingly, the admiration seemed to be mutual. Chris, though a liberal, hardly shared Redgrave's support of leftist causes. But getting to know her, he could see her as more than a name or political cipher, but as a person.

"There's an image of her over here of being completely humorless," he mused, "which is not at all true. She's childlike, warm, vulnerable, sweet, a person of great humanity, and one of the most gifted actresses in the world. In England her politics are not held against her [which was true only to an extent—she was seen as part of the "loony left"]; they accept her as the artist she is."

This being a Merchant-Ivory production, and the duo being long practiced at squeezing every dollar so tightly that it squeaked, it came in on time and on budget. Overruns couldn't happen; it was as simple and straightforward as that.

But for all the enforced parsimony, there was a real family atmosphere to the shoot. Every week, Merchant would cook Indian food for the cast, and at the wrap party everybody involved received a T-shirt emblazoned "I did it for curry." They were small gestures, but in the long run they counted for a great deal.

As did the reviews. *Playboy* deemed it "intelligent and impeccably made," if a little academic, which was more or less the same point that *Time* raised, although Richard Schickel did note that in Basil Ranson, Chris displayed "snaky masculine guile."

Maybe it was some subtle influence from Redgrave, or perhaps a greater concern for the world with his second child due at the end of the year, but after filming *The Bostonians,* Chris's own political conscience seemed to awaken.

He'd been so busy with career and family, as well as his recreational pursuits like flying, skiing, sailing, and music, that he hadn't given too much thought to the world at large. He'd been a member of the council for Actors' Equity, but that was directly involved with his profession.

Suddenly, almost out of the blue, he became involved with activists working to clean up the Hudson River and, in characteristic fashion, began to immerse himself in the science and legalities of the matter, grounding himself until he became something of an expert on the topic.

As Chris, Gae, and Matthew settled into Williamstown, and rehearsals for *Holiday* got under way, *Superman III* opened in theaters around the country. This time there was none of the trickery of premiering overseas before America. This was done in a straight-down-the-line, traditional manner. The Salkinds had spent a lot of money on the movie, and they desperately needed to recoup it. After the first weekend it seemed as if that wouldn't be a problem, with the film taking in a staggering $13 million.

And while it was a hit with moviegoers, eventually bringing in around $60 million—less than either of its predecessors, but still a very decent figure—it didn't fare too well with some of the critics, although a few genuinely enjoyed it. *Time* offered a very positive review, and most of that was directed at Chris's performance.

"Reeve brings both a light touch and sufficient muscle to Superman," Richard Corliss wrote. "And when he goes bad, he is a sketch of vice triumphant, swaggering towards the vixen Lorelei . . . for a sulfurous kiss. It is largely to Reeve's credit that this summer's moviegoers will look up at the screen and say, 'It's a hit . . . it's a delight . . . it's a super sequel.'"

And *Rolling Stone* felt it was "the funniest, liveliest and most original Superman movie yet," with Chris renewing "his vitality every time he plays the Man of Steel," while *The New Republic* called it "more amusing than expected."

Playboy praised Chris's work in the film, but thought the series was beginning "to show signs of strain."

In truth, beyond Chris the film had very little to recommend it. The first two movies, for all the problems surrounding them, seemed to have been crafted with love. As Chris had noted, this one seemed motivated solely by greed. The money had been spent to make it as lavish as possible, but it remained utterly devoid of any heart or soul.

It would be the last of Chris's youthful films, the final movie of his twenties. With his thirtieth birthday in 1982, it seemed as if a mantle of maturity had begun to settle around his shoulders, albeit uneasily at times. There would still be plenty of mistakes to be made, upheavals to be undergone, but he was beginning to grow into himself, to understand and accept that he'd never be fully able to shake off the image of "the guy in the boots," that he must integrate it into his personality rather than constantly fight it.

In many ways *The Bostonians* did him a service that *The Bounty* never could have. It not only allowed audiences to take him seriously as an actor (which even his excellent work in *Deathtrap* hadn't managed), it allowed him to take *himself* more seriously, to see how far he'd come, and how far he could go with all of this.

CHAPTER NINE

It was all well and good to have discovered these new ideals about acting and how to get the most out of himself as an actor. But there was always going to be a side to Chris that wasn't going to pass up the chance to self-indulge.

The only problem was that when the chance came, it placed him in a bind. He was offered the lead in a romantic adventure movie, *The Aviator,* which would allow him not only to fly—actually piloting a plane rather than moving through the skies in a blue suit—but also to do some second-unit direction. Those were the good points. The downside was that it would put him in Eastern Europe when his daughter was due to be born.

Understandably, it was a difficult decision to make. Being at Matthew's birth had been a huge experience for him, a bonding. At the same time, the chance to both fly and direct was remarkably tempting. And the script, from Ernest Gann's novel, was "deliberately romantic, old-fashioned family entertainment—the kind of film they don't make anymore."

That old-fashioned quality was also what had originally drawn him to *Somewhere in Time,* and he knew full well how that had turned out. This time, though, the director would be

George Miller, who'd done a good job on *The Man from Snowy River,* a film that combined action and sensitivity.

Finally, Chris opted to do the film; this first opportunity to direct couldn't be ignored. If it went well, it could offer another career option for the future, and being in charge of some of the second-unit shots wouldn't be too much responsibility for a beginner.

That's not to say that getting to fly an old biplane over Yugoslavia (where the location shooting would be done) didn't offer plenty of attractions of its own. There was no question of getting someone else for the flying and stunt sequences, even if the insurance necessary whenever Chris went aloft added a fair chunk to the budget.

Alexandra Reeve was born at Welbeck Hospital in London, exactly where her brother had come into the world four years earlier. Her father was able to fly home and be there when she was born, interrupting filming for this far more important event, and staying with Gae and the children for several days before rushing back to Eastern Europe to finish his work there.

His directorial debut was still to come. He'd expected standard second-unit material—the sort of background and establishing shots that would have been simple enough—but in the end he got something much meatier than that, a chance to direct himself.

His character, Edgar Anscombe, had crashed into a mountain in the middle of winter, and was forced to fight off a pack of wolves determined to make him into dinner. Those were the scenes Chris was given to work with—notably the coldest and most isolated of the whole film. As always, given the option, he wasn't going to use a stunt double.

"It wasn't really dangerous," he explained. "They were trained wolves; you can't get scared of animals with names like

Max and Ivan. All you do is hold a piece of chicken or meat in your hand, and on command they go for it."

In the end, though, for all its pleasures, being involved with *The Aviator* proved to be largely a waste of time. For a start, movies like this historically didn't really do well. *High Road to China,* a year or so earlier, had been fashioned as an aviation adventure vehicle for Tom Selleck (of *Magnum P.I.* fame), and hadn't exactly burst the studio coffers. For some reason, America didn't seem intrigued with the earlier days of flight, and adventure was only palatable when mixed with state-of-the-art special effects.

That was definitely part of the problem for *The Aviator,* and one which really should have been anticipated. The other was that George Miller had amazingly managed to make a boring film about flying, fighting wolves, and about a romance between Chris and Rosanna Arquette (who played an heiress). What emerged on-screen was little more than formulaic; even the action sequences seemed laid out by the numbers—the general consensus was that *The Aviator* simply didn't cut the mustard. There was no spark or sizzle. MGM-UA, who'd bankrolled it, agreed, and in the end it only found its way to a few theaters before quickly vanishing altogether. Reportedly, after seeing the final cut, Chris asked that it never be released, he was so displeased with it. He was having problems finding movies that would add to his luster.

But then again, how often had he been happy with the films he'd made? In *Superman* he had done a solid job, but he was young, still learning the ropes. He'd been pleased with his work in *Superman II, Deathtrap,* and *The Bostonians.* On the other hand, his work in *Somewhere in Time, Monsignor, Superman III,* and now *The Aviator* hadn't matched the standards he'd set for himself. Batting .500 might be excellent for baseball; for a movie actor those statistics didn't look so wonderful.

Perhaps it was that realization that made him decide to take a year off from movies. Some distance from the medium certainly wouldn't hurt, rather than working on slipshod productions that would end up doing his career no favors. He wanted to be able to spend time with his new daughter. And it wasn't as if he had no work lined up; 1984 was already fully booked, two-thirds of it with a return to what he loved best, stage work.

Vanessa Redgrave had apparently been very impressed with Chris's acting ability and his interpretation of Henry James. After completing filming on *The Bostonians,* she approached Chris about them working together again, in the West End this time, on a revival of *The Aspern Papers,* adapted from Henry James by Vanessa's father, Sir Michael Redgrave, who'd been largely responsible for the play first appearing in Shaftesbury Avenue, and she wanted to stage it as a tribute to him.

Of necessity, changes had to be made. A modern crowd of theatergoers would be less inclined to sit through a long production, so cuts had to be made. And Chris, at thirty-one, was much younger than Redgrave had been when he played Henry Jarvis, so some revisions were also in order there.

Rehearsals, understandably, took place in London in early 1984, so Chris, Gae, Matthew, and Alexandra, barely a month old then, found themselves shuttling back across the Atlantic and settling into their London house for a few months.

The timing was perfect for Chris. The relative routine of a theatrical play meant he could be home every night with his family, offering support to a slightly frazzled Gae. Rehearsals lasted the length of winter, from January until the beginning of March, followed by a tryout quite a way out of town—in sunny Monaco.

Initially, Chris's presence seemed to be on sufferance from the rest of the cast and crew. Being British, they knew him not from his stage work, but from his movies, and that left them dubious about his ability, to say the least, in spite of all Redgrave's recommendations.

The play's director, Frith Banbury, offered him a backhanded compliment by saying that "anyone who has the guts to come to London to play this difficult part is to be admired and congratulated."

It didn't take long to win them over, however. As he'd shown in *The Bostonians,* Chris seemed to have a natural affinity for Henry James—they'd both, after all, been born in New York and enjoyed privileged, Ivy League educations—which melded well with his natural talents. The ensemble, which also included the remarkable Dame Wendy Hiller, came together quickly around the script and were ready for the opening at the Theatre Royal on March 8, 1984.

The play was excellently received, as it had every right to be, but the surprise for the English reviewers was how good Chris was. Based on his movie work (*The Bostonians* would not be released until later that year), it had been anticipated that he'd fall flat on his face in such exalted company, but he more than held his own. The *Daily Telegraph* put it simply, writing, "He can act!" but other papers offered more in-depth assessments of his work onstage.

In *The New Statesman,* he was praised for a "charisma [and] a ruthlessness that is both repellent and fascinating."

The *Observer* noted in particular a moment in the play when Jarvis seemed to pounce "as if Henry Jarvis were so eager to get at the papers of Jeffrey Aspern that he forgets himself at the last moment and positively runs up the final steps to take the unwitting defenders by surprise.

"It is, physically and psychologically, a marvelous moment and compels in an audience anxious to clap whatever they can, a chilled and electrifying silence. The barbarians are no longer at the gates. Mr. Reeve remains watchable throughout."

This time there was no talk of being wooden at the beginning of the run. Everything clicked perfectly from the opening night onward for the entire length of the production, so perfectly that there was even talk of a film version using the same cast, although all the studios approached considered the venture to be just too risky, meaning that, to Chris's disappointment, in the end the venture had to be abandoned.

But the play was exactly the type of triumph and ego boost that Chris needed, particularly as it was followed by the opening of *The Bostonians,* which brought him even more glowing reviews.

Suddenly, instead of looking like someone starting on the slippery slope to obscurity, he was back with a fresh bloom on the rose and a rising reputation for the quality of his work. He even seemed to be formulating a plan for his career, claiming that he wanted to make two movies a year, in spring and fall, one serious, one a comedy, to show all the facets of his acting personality. That would leave summer free for Williamstown, the place that seemed to constantly renew him, and winter to be with his family and enjoy skiing, a sport he hadn't had much opportunity to practice recently.

Even if he didn't reestablish himself as a star of the magnitude he'd been at the end of the 1970s, he'd still be doing what he loved and making a comfortable, if not extravagant, living. That would put him ahead of 99 percent of the people in his profession. And he'd be better off for it. He'd had a large dose of star status, enough to know that it didn't sit too comfortably on him. He was more concerned with acting than image, and finally, it appeared, he was establishing a level for himself.

Williamstown was the place that called him when *The Aspern Papers* ended its run in June. The family picked up and relocated back to Massachusetts, where Chris would be taking the lead in A. R. Gurney's *Richard Corey.*

As usual, the two-month run seemed like a vacation. He could spend his days relaxing with Gae and the kids, sailing, flying, walking the baby, without autograph seekers stopping him on the streets of the small town.

The play was remarkably well received and he was offered the chance to play the title role on Broadway, but in his new maturity he declined.

"I'm sure it would go," he said, "but I'm not sure it would be satisfying to me. It was such a perfect little production at Williamstown. There was a time when I was struggling to show my range, but now I'm past all that. I don't need to come and show off on Broadway."

On the surface it seemed like an odd statement from someone who, just four years earlier, had regarded acting in *Fifth of July* on the Great White Way to be something of a career pinnacle. But there were a couple of things to be considered. Chris was coming off six straight months of theater, both rehearsals and performances; he needed a change, something different. But perhaps more important was the fact that he'd already played Broadway in a lead role. It was a challenge he'd conquered, just as, to his own satisfaction, he'd already conquered *Richard Corey.* To have kept on doing that would have been akin to standing still, and Chris always needed to be moving forward.

One challenge he'd hoped for was a role in *Children of a Lesser God,* but that didn't happen. Instead there was an opportunity to do something lavish in the medium he'd been brought up to think of as second-class—a television movie.

But it wasn't any of the standard "disease of the week" vehicles. This would be as lavish as anything Hollywood had come up with lately, a pull-out-all-the-stops adaptation of Tolstoy's *Anna Karenina.*

In September 1984 West was West and East was still East. The chances of an American cast and crew filming the story in its native Russia were nil. Instead they found the next best place, also in Eastern Europe, but with a much more liberal attitude, where the landscape and the buildings still looked right, and the locals were pleased to work cheaply—Hungary. And that was where Chris went in September to begin the filming. It

Christopher Reeve was on top of the world when he moved to New York City—young, single, and successful. (Nancy Barr/Retna Ltd.)

At Juilliard, Christopher perfected his craft and roomed with future megastar Robin Williams. (Jim Demetropoulos/Retna Ltd.)

Christopher and Juilliard buddy Kevin Kline were both presenters at the 1985 Obie Awards, Off-Broadway's Tony Awards. (Walter McBride/Retna Ltd.)

Christopher with the two women in his life—*Superman's* "Lois Lane" (Margot Kidder) and Gae Exton, his then live-in lover and the mother of his two eldest children. (Richard Young/Retna Ltd.)

Superman with his female counterpart, *Supergirl* star Helen Slater, at the premiere of *Superman III*. (Richard Young/Retna Ltd.)

(Above) In addition to the role that made him famous, Christopher also starred in a number of serious, literary dramas, including *The Bostonians*. (Camera Press/Retna Ltd.)

(Left) Christopher and the new Mrs. Reeve, Dana Morosoni, beam for the camera. (Steve Douglas/Retna Ltd.)

(Left) Since the accident, Christopher has lobbied tirelessly for additional funding for increased spinal-injury research. He was an inspirational speaker at the Democratic National Convention.
(Patsy Lynch/Retna Ltd.)

(Below) Christopher fulfilled his dream of directing with *In the Gloaming,* starring Glenn Close.
(I.P.A. Stills/Retna Ltd.)

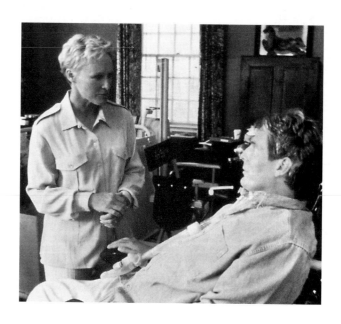

Dana and their son Will congratulate Christopher on being awarded a star on Hollywood's Walk of Fame. (Steve Granitz/Retna Ltd.)

Whatever the future brings, Christopher and Dana will face it together. (Marissa Roth/Retna Ltd.)

was his third period drama in a little over twelve months (and obviously his "serious" project for the year), but oddly there was no mention of him being typecast in that manner the way there had been as Superman.

But in Budapest, at least, Superman was one thing he didn't have to worry about, since the movies had never been released there. By an ironic quirk of fate, however, *Deathtrap* had, which meant that "the people in the street, when they do recognize me, think of me as a gay psychotic playwright and leave me alone."

With his fame not preceding him for once, Chris was free to get on with the job in hand. This version of *Anna Karenina* should have had everything going for it. The cast, with the exception of Chris as Count Vronsky, was entirely British. Jacqueline Bissett had the title role, and the other lead was Paul Scofield, who'd won an Oscar for his performance in *A Man for All Seasons.* James Goldman, who'd penned *The Lion in Winter,* had written the script, while Simon Langton, whose television credits included *Smiley's People,* was the director. In short, it was employing the crème de la crème.

Chris's first exposure to the world of television movies surprised him, even more than his time with Merchant-Ivory. With just $5 million to spend, he quickly learned that "the budget is the budget. You can't steal one more minute than you're allotted."

He'd originally discovered the book when he was at Cornell, calling it "a page-turner, compelling reading . . . possibly one of the best novels ever written," which was only apt, given Franklin Reeve's specialization in Russian literature. The quality of the story was what made him want to be a part of it, even though he'd be playing second fiddle to Bissett, who was, in reality, a lesser star in the pantheon than he was.

"I just think, 'Will I be enjoying this part?' " he asked himself, and the answer was a large yes.

Both Chris and Bissett had their own ways of working, and on such a tight schedule, with little time allowed for rehearsal, that caused problems.

"You don't get much from me at rehearsal," Bissett admitted in *TV Guide.* "I resist being overfocused. . . . Chris needs to talk about things a great deal. His working process is more tortured than mine. He needs to know a zillion details before he focuses."

Chris wanted the cast to work together in rehearsals, "to explore the characters, to dig into the script," he said. "[Bissett's] way of working is to get it together on her own, which can be disconcerting to actors who are used to a different method."

All of which reportedly led to tension between the pair, although neither would openly admit it. In fact, in public they were perfectly amicable; in the same interview, Chris went out of his way to praise her as someone who was "always on time and word-perfect in scenes. She's a top-drawer professional."

The shoot itself was an exercise in exhaustion. Much of the money for *Anna Karenina* had gone on its stars and the costumes, more than three thousand of them, which had been rented from Moscow and London. It was going to look grand, gorgeous, and extravagant. However, that translated into long, long days on the sets and locations, with fifteen setups a day being the rule rather than the exception (in Hollywood five would have seemed a huge load). The fact that virtually three-quarters of the crew were Hungarian didn't speed things along, since everything had to be translated for them. And the local technical standards were well below those of their Western colleagues.

"The people are all warm and friendly, but there is a language barrier," Chris said. "There's also a lack of expertise."

One other problem in working for television was the network censors, people he'd never encountered before.

"In one scene, Chris was supposed to kiss the top of my cleavage, but the TV censors said it wouldn't wash," Bissett remembered.

"No kissing below the neck. This put the kibosh on one of the scenes we were in the middle of," Chris agreed with a laugh. "I was just about to make my move, and got pulled back." But in some ways he was grateful for the restrictions, since it allowed the audiences to focus on the story, rather than the sex.

"It's a distortion to make a classic novel play like *Dallas*," he asserted. "That's putting twentieth-century audience needs on top of the reality of the piece. In our piece the implications are made, but we don't cut to a bedroom to interest the audience."

Titillation was definitely not the order of the day, and that meshed well with Chris's views on the entire production.

"Our primary function is to entertain and make an intelligent story. But if it causes twenty people to want to run and pick up the novel and study it, I think that would be great. . . . You don't have to play down to the lowest common denominator. You don't have to play it down to the eleven-year-old mind. So much of television plays it down and, not being snobbish about it, how nice it is to have something that doesn't."

Unlike film, where there could be a gap of a year between the shoot finishing and the premiere, time is very much of the essence in every aspect of television. The last takes of *Anna Karenina* had taken place in November 1984. On March 26, 1985, before Chris had even got another role, it was aired on CBS. The reactions, as usual for anything major attempted by an American network, were mixed.

USA Today had kind words for Chris, noting that "Reeve's Vronsky has the perfect pitch of the lovelorn naif—youthfulness, extravagance, and crass opportunism," and the *Christian Science Monitor* conceded that "he finally manages to integrate his own cool persona into a fairly believable Vronsky."

But the *New York Times* didn't see things through such rose-colored lenses. John O'Connor felt that "all done up in splendid military costumes, Mr. Reeve is indeed handsome, but rather distressingly lifeless. He seems to be devoting most of his energy to maintaining a reasonably accurate British accent. He ends up being the nineteenth-century equivalent of a big lug."

Even *People* had little pleasant to say, calling it, at best "a tepid tale of love," and Chris's acting "to passion what kryptonite is to Superman."

Unremarkably, it didn't fare particularly well in the ratings. It seemed that the only times the Americans could offer any seal of approval to costume dramas were when they came from England and were aired on *Masterpiece Theater.* At the same time, it was true that Americans, however much care and money they took, were unable to offer the same subtleties as those British productions, and that anything made for the three networks was almost certainly the kiss of death for a classic, since it almost always had to be reduced to its lowest common denominators.

Chris had his plan for two movies a year, but for it to work he actually needed to get two roles a year, and after *Anna Karenina* there wasn't another one in sight. *The Running Man* had gone to Arnold Schwarzenegger, leaving him with no immediate prospects.

Although *The Bostonians* had done well in reviews and, because of its tiny budget, made a healthy profit, it was an art film and discounted by the big studios. That meant his last major role (not including *The Aviator,* which had never seen general release) had been in *Superman III,* which was now a couple of years old. Whereas after the first two movies in the *Superman* series the offers had come in thick and fast, all tinkling with very healthy chunks of change, now he was having to pursue roles, and finding difficulty in securing them. Chris *knew* he was still doing good work, and that he'd given some excellent performances in the past, but Hollywood wasn't coming calling anymore. He'd stopped being hot. Away from the cape and boots, Chris wasn't a big box-office draw.

Much of that was due to himself. His independent streak had come home to roost. After years of turning down the big-budget films, with their ridiculous salaries, the studios were finally believing that he simply wasn't interested. Maybe he'd said no often enough for it to have finally sunk in.

There were plenty of other options available to him, of course. There was theater, and, now that he'd broken the barrier, more television. And by the mid-eighties, other work was available for jobbing actors, like reading audio books. Even if it didn't quite have the same glamour as flying over Metropolis, it was acting, after a fashion.

And it was a paycheck, which was becoming a serious consideration. Chris might never have considered himself a "movie star" as such, but he'd never stinted himself on movie star's luxuries. With Gae, he had homes in New York, Los Angeles, and London, three airplanes, and a sailboat. These were the privileges of a wealthy man, and it took a certain income level to maintain the standard of life Chris had achieved.

Now, finding himself not heavily sought after for the lucrative movie roles, he had two choices: scale back on his lifestyle or go for anything and everything that was available, no matter what it was.

Within limits, he chose the latter. He'd work hard, make what he needed, but there were also acting jobs he'd take because he wanted to do them, regardless of the income they brought.

The family's yearly sojourn in Williamstown would always be one of those. Nineteen eighty-five saw them back again for July and August, while Chris starred in *The Royal Family.* Performing even gave him a new idea: He'd briefly tried his hand at directing in *The Aviator*. Maybe it was possible to combine that with his love of theater?

"I'd like to take a good five-character play with a lot of emotional detail and work on that," he suggested. "I think I have the eye for it, and I feel I could really bridge the gap between the actor and the audience."

However, it seemed that no one was listening. No directing jobs were offered.

On the other hand, there was plenty of television work available, and Reeve reached for it, narrating a special called *Dinosaur!* and one much closer to his heart, *Juilliard at 80,* for which he was a perfectly justifiable choice, being one of its more famous alumni, albeit not a graduate.

By the autumn of 1985, he was back working in New York theater. It wasn't Broadway, or anything close. In fact, Circle in the Square's production of *The Marriage of Figaro* was unlike anything Chris had been involved in before. It was decidedly avant-garde, and he admitted that "it's a totally different kind of theater than I'm used to—that's why I wanted to be a part of it.

"My own hope for my life is that I never chicken out. I'd like to keep feeling reckless about things and having that roller-coaster ride of up/down, success/failure—anything but play it safe."

With *The Marriage of Figaro,* playing it safe was something he could never have been accused of. His was essentially a comedic role in a production that seemed to resemble a car wreck more than anything coherent, and unsurprisingly, according to the critics, it seemed to fall on that down/failure side of the roller coaster, as critic Frank Rich noted when he wrote, "His efforts at clowning sink with the finality of pure lead."

But that was the risk he'd taken, and at least he'd been willing to take it. Chris had made some dubious choices of roles in his career, but he'd always been willing to go out on a limb for something he believed in, regardless of how little it might advance his career. He'd done everything with a great deal of integrity, and that meant more to him than any amount of money.

The Marriage of Figaro didn't enjoy a particularly long run, and when it was over, Chris once again found himself at a loose end. There were roles being discussed, but nothing definite set, no contracts signed or checks in the mail.

It was a disconcerting, slightly disorienting period. There was no danger of him being finished as an actor, but after so many years of constant employment the lull was strange, not so much a vacation as a limbo, and one which did nothing to stave off his increasing financial worries.

His spirits couldn't have been helped by the fact that he and Gae seemed to be growing apart. With his work, they'd never been like a normal couple, spending every night together, but they'd grabbed their days with each other whenever they could and made the most of them.

Now she was spending more time in London with the kids, while Chris seemed to pass most of his months in America. She had her business, which was doing well, and seemed to be developing a full life away from him. Matthew, now six years old, was enrolled in an expensive private school in England, which meant that Gae couldn't just pick up and leave whenever the whim took her. She was becoming more firmly anchored to a life lived, more or less, in one place, and most of the time that life didn't seem to include Chris. He had characterized her as "fundamentally a practical person . . . organized, focused in terms of common sense, always looking for the logic in things." But as a parent who was often alone and a businesswoman, she had to be.

On the other hand, he quite perceptively saw himself as "a

romantic, a dreamer. . . . I blow hot and cold. I'm also transparent. I can't fake anything, whereas Gae can sometimes hold back emotions. For an actor, I'm a lousy actor."

The couple had been together for eight years, but now it seemed as if they were slowly and inexorably beginning to drift away from each other. The tabloids had been predicting that for a long time, but in the past they'd always shown themselves to be stronger than rumor. At the same time, it wasn't over yet. The signs were all there, but there was still a chance for Chris and Gae to salvage things before they went too far.

The situation would certainly be improved if Chris could take care of his money worries, if serendipity would work in his favor and give him the kind of lump sum he'd been turning down a few years before. With that off his mind, he'd be able to focus on other matters.

CHAPTER TEN

The gods were obviously on his side. There was a big payday coming, and from the source he'd least expected—Superman. After the third movie had been so severely savaged by the critics, the Salkinds had sold off the film rights and quit while they were still ahead.

They'd been picked up by Menahem Golem and Yoram Globus, who owned the Cannon Group. Their reputation was for producing low-budget films of not especially outstanding quality, specializing in the type of Chuck Norris bloodfests that had been so popular.

Their movies never approached art, even from a distance, but they did have a consistent knack for ending up in the black, and since the bottom line was far more important than the content, the Cannon Group was quite successful.

Now they were going to put their particular polish on Superman, and they wanted Chris to reprise his twin roles.

After the debacle of *Superman III* he'd declared he'd never play the character again, and he meant it. But that was then, and this was now. Other producers weren't knocking down his door with offers. *The Aviator* remained a skeleton in his closet, which meant that he hadn't had a movie released for three years, since 1983's *The Bostonians*. Stage work and television were fine, but a film was high-profile; he needed something that would get his name back out in front of the public, and in turn bring in more scripts.

A film was also money, and what Cannon was offering matched the amount he'd made for *Superman III*.

Chris would have gladly accepted that, since no one else was bidding for his services, but his agent decided it was time to begin some real wheeling and dealing, and get Chris the type of fee he should have had all along for Superman, as well as any other conditions he might want to impose.

That he got everything he wanted was no surprise. When the Salkinds had briefly considered a *Superman IV*, they'd claimed, "The public is most interested in the character, not in the actor. If we find the right actor for the part, we'll make the movie with him."

But there was only one actor, and that was Chris; he was *perfect* for the part. He was the person the public knew and loved, whom they associated with the role. Anyone else would have been a poor substitute at best, and that would have been reflected at the box office.

So, for the first time in his life, even though he wasn't one any longer, Chris got to realize the full power of the big-time Hollywood actor. He would have script approval, he'd be able to direct some of the second-unit shots (as he had on *The Aviator*), and most artistically gratifying of all, for Chris agreeing to make *Superman IV*, Cannon would finance another picture of Chris's choice—to be made *before* the epic.

And on top of all that he'd receive $4 million.

It was big money, but totaled up, it meant that Chris had still made less than $7 million for playing the Man of Steel four times, not the kind of figure to put him in stratospheric company.

Still, this was a very sweet deal. The money worries were off his back, and he had not one, but two projects he could sink his teeth into. One for himself, one for the bank account. For his "own" movie, he picked *Street Smart,* a fact-based drama about a New York journalist who invented his stories. The screenplay had been written by the journalist in question, David Freeman, a freelance writer who'd once concocted a story about a pimp for *New York* magazine.

Unfortunately, a real pimp who bore a strong resemblance to the writer's invention had been arrested for murder, and his lawyer decided to subpoena the journalist's notes—which, naturally, didn't exist. To protect himself, and not reveal the truth, the journalist was forced to stand on his First Amendment rights, and that was where the problems really began. . . .

Chris had been interested in the script a few years before, when it was called "Streets of New York," and now, rewritten, it was brought to his attention again (both Reeve and Freeman had the same agent at ICM, Jim Wiatt).

Making *Street Smart* before *Superman IV* was a clever move. It meant there was no danger of the big picture being made and then Cannon backing out of the smaller one. And it allowed Chris to get his indulgence out of his system first, before he got down to the lucrative work. With its small budget of $3 million, if it didn't make money, Cannon could easily absorb the loss; they stood to make plenty from Superman.

"The central character (Jonathan Fisher) is not likable and definitely not a hero," Chris explained about his pet project. "But he's like many people in their mid-thirties, facing a dilemma of personal ethics versus ambition. He's sort of lost, just getting along, but he wants to be famous. When he gets the opportunity, he takes it."

In other words, he saw a few reflections of himself in Fisher. After all, Chris was himself in his mid-thirties, and trying hard to balance art and commerce, "just getting along."

"Life is not about good guys and bad guys. It's about people trying to survive, it's about personal ethics versus the pressure to succeed. I felt it would be interesting to play a man who is really quite lost, very weak, dishonest, and stupid in many ways."

Now, more mature, with a few lines adding character to his face, Chris was really old enough to attempt a role like this. If he'd done it at the height of his fame it would have seemed a deliberate attempt to erase the Superman image. Now it seemed like nothing more than an actor coming to grips with good material.

For his research into the world of pimps and hookers he spent a couple of weeks with the NYPD vice squad, patrolling, being present at arrests, and talking to the women plying their trade out on the street.

"A lot of the girls recognized me from films," he told the *New York Daily News,* "and were excited not only to talk to me but to proposition me. At a discount. I also had some freebie offers, which is saying a lot, and some interesting combination offers."

Chris, however, kept his virtue intact, although he readily admitted, "There is some very attractive talent down there." He had a picture to make, and not much money with which to do it. Jerry Schatzberg was picked to direct, and a remarkably strong supporting cast was assembled, as Morgan Freeman, Mimi Rogers, and Kathy Baker all signed on to the project, with the legendary Miles Davis providing the music.

Since this was very much Chris's baby, he took a hands-on role throughout. He worked with Freeman on the script, and stayed on the sets for hours. Even illness couldn't stop him. After an emergency appendectomy forced him into the hospital, he was back at work two days later, getting to grips with a fight scene.

Street Smart was definitely gritty, exactly as Chris had hoped. The problem, as with much of the other work he was proud of, was that hardly anyone saw it. Cannon had agreed to finance it, but distribution was another matter. With its very dark subject matter and a decided lack of action sequences, it was never a very marketable proposition, far more art than commerce—something well out of Cannon's depth. In the end it was shown in a few places, but like *The Aviator* (although for completely different reasons) it never saw general release.

Those few showings were enough, however. Chris had taken on the challenge of surrounding himself with quality acting talent, and in the end—perhaps because he was trying to do too much on this film—they shone more strongly than he did. Morgan Freeman, in particular, turned in sterling work, enough to walk away with four awards as a supporting actor, and an Oscar nomination in the same category, while Baker got one award as supporting actress.

Chris fared nowhere near as well. For him there were no awards, and precious little praise, which must have been particularly galling after giving so much of himself to the film.

In *The New Yorker,* Pauline Kael liked much of the film, but not the screenplay with its "thin, brassy attitudes," and she remained unimpressed by Chris, who she felt was "physically too inexpressive to play inexpressiveness; it isn't the character who's a lug—it's Reeve." *People* wasn't convinced by any of the movie, and Peter Travers wrote that it "should be sentenced to cable TV, followed quickly by obscurity."

As soon as *Street Smart* was through postproduction, Chris had to attend to his other obligation, *Superman IV.* The idea for the script had largely originated with him, and reflected his new concerns with world peace.

"We're going for something emotional," he told AP. "Ultimately we would all like to see a world without nuclear weapons. The question is, why can't somebody just take them away?"

That somebody, of course, would be Superman. But Chris certainly wasn't in shape to lift one nuclear weapon, let alone the global arsenal of them. He hadn't let himself go to seed, but now that he was well past thirty his physique no longer resembled the Man of Steel's, either. There was plenty of working out, both mental and physical, to be done before filming began at Cannon's Elstree Studio in England.

At least he could be with Gae and the kids (both Matthew and Alexandra would be in the film), although the relationship was far from what it had once been. The time apart, and the way they'd grown in different directions, had put strains on their love that were finally beginning to look irreversible. After the way it had all begun with a bang, it looked as if, almost ten years later, it was going to end with a whimper.

Not just yet, though. For the moment they were still together, or as together as they could be when Chris was in the middle of filming. With his demands all met, he had a lot of responsibility for this movie, working on the script with writers Lawrence Kohner and Mark Rosenthal. Beyond the basic idea of Superman gathering up the world's nuclear armaments and throwing them into the sun, he even penned a few of the scenes himself, as well as undertaking a great deal of the second-unit direction.

In theory, *Superman IV: The Quest for Peace,* as it was to be known, should have seen a return to the standards of the first two films in the series. Gene Hackman was back to play Lex Luthor again, Jackie Cooper had returned, and Margot Kidder had Superman as her boyfriend again, while Mariel Hemingway had a turn as Clark Kent's love interest.

That was the theory, at least. The reality was that while Cannon wanted a big-budget movie, they weren't prepared for it, and the production quite literally ran out of money five months before everything was due to be finished.

It left both cast and crew in limbo. Instead of something classy and entertaining, the scenes which still had to be completed ended up being shot cheaply and shoddily.

For the want of investing a little more money, Cannon would end up paying the price many times over once the film was released. And not only Cannon. For everyone involved it looked like this was going to be a disaster, but for none more so than Chris.

He'd end up with his money, which was the ultimate reason he'd undertaken to play "the guy in the boots" one last time, and the movie he wanted had been made, but he certainly didn't need to suffer the indignity of walking away from all this with his reputation in tatters.

"The movie was his idea and the idea was great," said Jon Cryer, who played a criminal in it, "and the shooting was great, and Gene Hackman was doing wonderful improvisational stuff— I loved working with him—and then Cannon ran out of money . . . and released an unfinished movie. . . . They used the same flying shot like four times. That was the problem with it, and that's why Chris leveled with me and said, 'It's a mess.' And I said, 'Oh, great.' "

Chris had been so closely involved that it would be impossible for him to disavow this one. His name was all over it. The best he could manage was to finish his work to the best of his ability and move on, which is precisely what he did, completing the filming in June and immediately flying back to Massachusetts for another summer season with the Williamstown Theatre, this time in *Summer and Smoke*.

For once, though, he undertook the journey alone, and spent the summer by himself, while Gae and the kids remained in London. The fractures in the relationship were there, worse than they had been; it was over in everything but name.

Williamstown was the place he felt comfortable, a sort of spiritual home, and in his solitude he determined to make it a physical home as well, spending just over a quarter of a million dollars to buy a farm in the Berkshires, on the New York–Massachusetts border.

In many ways he found a real bargain, although he'd end up spending another hundred thousand dollars on the property over the next couple of years. It was more modern manor than farmhouse, two stories, with five bedrooms and six and a half baths, constructed of wood, pine and cherry inside, cedar shingles outside.

"The house is facing the wrong way for the view," he said expansively, "so I'm adding a wing and dabbling in landscaping—put an orchard here, move the pond there."

And the acreage was exactly what he needed for all his indulgences: "I can park my glider, and there's a cross-country ski run, livestock, a trout stream."

He'd finally joined the landed gentry, but doing it on his own meant that in the main it was a lonely summer, broken only when he was contacted by U.S. senator Patrick Leahy, who was hoping for Chris's support on the campaign trail in the upcoming 1986 election.

Chris was surprised, and probably a little flattered. It wasn't unusual for actors to lend their names to political causes—indeed, it was a time when a former actor was in the White House—but his real political involvement had been minimal. He had his own beliefs and he'd worked with the Hudson River conservation group, but that was as far as his commitment extended.

Chris wasn't about to lend his name to anything or anyone without doing his homework. He discovered that Leahy was, like himself, a liberal Democrat, one who'd opposed aid to the contras in Nicaragua. He was a staunch environmentalist. If his name could be of any use, Chris was prepared to let him use it, and once the summer season in Williamstown was over, he even went up to Vermont to make campaign appearances on Leahy's behalf, making speeches, signing autographs, and appearing at fund-raisers.

A good deal of that was a genuine wish to help. But it was also a way of filling time. There was no family to return to, and for the moment he had no work waiting—he might even have wondered if he'd ever work again once the world saw the debacle known as the new Superman movie. This way he could at least channel his energy in a positive direction.

Gratifyingly, it worked: Leahy kept his seat in the November election. But that was the only high spot as winter came rolling in. After a series of long-distance conversations, he and Gae agreed there was nothing to be salvaged in their relationship, and that the best thing was just to put an end to it. There were the children to be considered, however. They'd live with Gae and be brought up in England, but they'd still spend time with Chris whenever schedules permitted.

"I trust the communication between Gae and me will be good enough so that we can work out whatever's best for the kids," Chris finally explained to *McCall's* in the wake of it all. "For now, they understand they have two homes, and they'll be fully loved and accepted in each."

It was all perfectly civilized, but sad. One thing it wasn't was public. These were their private lives, the kind of dirty laundry no one else needed to see, and it would be another six months, after repeated press inquiries, until any kind of statement about the breakup was issued.

Even then Chris was reluctant to talk about it. The *McCall's* interview was the only time he'd even go into detail about the end of the relationship, in spite of all the speculation in the tabloids (who, in the summer of 1987, had him dumping Gae for the kids' baby-sitter, Dana Morosini; in fact, she and Chris had only just met that year, and Chris's split with Gae had happened months before).

Nor did he leave Gae in the lurch; Chris was too much of a gentleman for that. With part of his recent *Superman* money, he bought a house in London for her and the children, so they'd have a solid base. Legends was doing well for her, making money, and though she had to work hard to keep it going and raise a family alone, the years of Chris frequently gone on location had made her no stranger to that.

"There was never an incident, never an act of cruelty or a betrayal between Gae and me," Chris said. "It was just a growing awareness that we were the wrong people for each other. It's not sugary and fake, but we're friends. That's really all there is to say. That is the whole truth."

Still, it was a bleak period for Chris. He had no partner, the movie on which he'd staked so much of his reputation seemed certain to be a critical and commercial failure, and there was no lucrative work on the horizon, beyond the opportunity to narrate a documentary called *Future Flight;* at least the subject was close to his heart.

His plan to make two movies a year had perforce gone by the board. He could only make them if he was offered the roles, and the phone simply wasn't ringing the way it once had. It was as if Christopher Reeve had gone out of fashion. His reputation was still intrinsically sound, but, outside of *Superman,* his name just didn't set the cash registers tinkling, and what Hollywood wanted in its male leads were proven box-office draws. The studios were no longer in business to walk the artistic edges. It didn't really matter how good or how bad the actors were in the roles. It didn't even matter if the movies themselves were awful, as long as the finished product looked slick and the crowds kept coming. With stars, writers, everybody demanding more money, and the spiraling cost of all those special effects the public seemed to lap up, the studios were less and less willing to take chances. Chris might have been able to act rings around many of the men whose names were appearing above the titles, but it was becoming less and less likely he'd have the opportunity.

By reappearing as Superman he'd done his wallet a big favor, but in the long term he'd hurt his career—not merely because of *Superman IV*'s lack of quality (although he knew that wasn't going to help him), but because he'd become associated with his character yet again. It had been one of those pairings that had been so perfect from the beginning that he'd never be able to leave it behind entirely, but coming back again just reinforced it in the mass consciousness.

So when a movie offer came along, he grabbed it with both hands. The money was welcome, but far more important was working again. He wasn't a star in this, but that didn't matter. The order in which the names appeared was important to some actors, but not Chris. Here was a chance to exercise his comedic muscles, playing a none too bright rich man, Blaine Bingham, in *Switching Channels*.

The story itself was far from new. It had started movie life in 1931 as *The Front Page* (and even then it was an adaptation of a stage play) and had then become *His Girl Friday,* and it seemed to get dusted off and taken out every few years for a remake, each one adding a slight twist to the original.

This variation offered Kathleen Turner as the female lead, a television news anchorwoman working for her ex-husband, played by Burt Reynolds (making this version something like *The Front Page* crossed with *The Mary Tyler Moore Show*). Chris was her hopeful suitor, a sporting goods manufacturer, eventually rejected in favor of career.

Inspired was one thing it wasn't, and Chris with dyed blond

hair was a sight that just didn't look right. However, he insisted he enjoyed the role.

"Blaine is such a weenie," he announced, "but I got a kick out of playing him because he's different."

And indeed he was. Chris played Bingham as someone closer to Clark Kent than any Superman, more caricature than character, and *Time* would say in its review that "Christopher Reeve brings a new macho wimpitude to the role of [Turner's] new beau—he's Clark Kent with a preening ego." Even *Playboy* liked him, calling him "the movie's happiest surprise, playing a sort of Ken-doll character and fine-tuning the sophisticated comic flair he brought to Superman."

The filming was quick, smooth, on time and on budget, but then again, these were all seasoned professionals without the need for any prima donna antics. They all knew the drill—just turn in the best performance possible and move on to the next project.

"I really did that movie just to fool around," Chris said. "I thought it could work, but it was played much too broadly. None of the characters were vulnerable enough to get much sympathy, and you ended up not caring about anybody."

Had he really taken it "just to fool around"? Given that he wasn't being showered with offers, it seemed unlikely. He'd become what he'd originally set out to be—a jobbing actor, working at whatever was on offer as long as it kept him in the business and paid the bills. The promise of a decade before, and the big roles and big money he'd refused, weren't about to be repeated.

"I've become philosophical about it," he admitted. "There have been so many highs and lows, and I don't always want to take the roller-coaster ride anymore."

That might have sounded like an admission of defeat, but by spring 1987, Chris was weary. After he'd completed *Switching Channels,* once again there were no more movie offers waiting. In fact, beyond Williamstown, there was nothing at all. It would be four years before he'd work in a cinematic film again.

With no work, and no family to console him, he returned to Williamstown for their 1987 season. There, at least, was a feeling of comfort, surrounded by people he knew—many of whom he'd worked with every summer for years—and who accepted him for who he was. Onstage in Williamstown he might be on show, but it was his retreat from the world.

CHAPTER ELEVEN

That season he was due to play in *The Rover* at Williamstown. It wasn't a lead, merely support, a fairly easy, gentle passage through the summer. Emotionally, his life was slowly beginning to come back together, even if things still looked fairly bleak professionally.

He'd gone to Williamstown in June to begin rehearsals and relax on the farm, and on the thirtieth of the month went down with friends to the 1896 House, a cabaret, for a few drinks and a chance to relax and catch up.

At a first, quick glance, he must have thought the woman who climbed onstage to sing "The Music That Makes Me Dance" was Gae; there was a strong resemblance between them. Both were tall, with long, shiny dark hair, and leggy. And he was still very susceptible to any woman who reminded him of the person with whom he'd spent almost ten years, the mother of his children.

When her set was finished, immediately attracted, Chris introduced himself, and discovered that her name was Dana Morosini, and invited her out to an after-hours club. At first she refused.

"My friends were telling me, 'You're crazy. Give us your keys.

He wants to give you a ride!' " she recalled, "and I said, 'Well, I have a car, I can get there on my own.' "

Chris finally persuaded her to follow him to the club, and there, he remembered, "We ended up talking for an hour. We didn't get a drink, we didn't sit down, we didn't move. Everything just vanished around us."

Dana was intrigued by him, but it was anything but love at first sight for her. Chris was smitten, but she remained guarded. She wasn't about to jump into something with a man who was essentially still on the rebound. After a quick kiss on the cheek, she left and went home—alone.

At twenty-six, she was enjoying her first season in Williamstown. She wasn't cast in the "big" play, but in another, smaller one, as well as doing other work around the festival, anything to keep her close to the theater.

Like Chris, Dana Charles Morosini had a fairly privileged background. She was born in New Jersey; her father was a doctor, and her mother worked in publishing. As a child, the family had moved to the New York suburb of Westchester County, an area where wealth was the norm, and Dana was a normal child, a bit of a tomboy who ended up doing chores like chopping wood. She learned to ride, but discovered she enjoyed singing and acting in school plays at Edgemont High School.

That was where the acting bug entered her system. After graduation she moved on to Yale, to study drama under Nikos Psacharopoulos, the man who was also the artistic director at the Williamstown Theatre. She took part in the usual student productions and attended all the commercial auditions she could, but without much success. And once she'd got her degree she headed west.

Not to try her luck in Los Angeles and the world of movies and television, however, but to pursue a more academic life, studying for an M.F.A. at the prestigious California Institute of the Arts, more or less a Left Coast version of Juilliard.

With her master's in her hand, Dana Morosini returned to New York. Her love was stage work, and to pursue that she really needed to be in Manhattan. But it wasn't easy. There were small roles in Off-Off-Broadway shows that hardly anyone attended, in places the big reviewers would never venture. The highlight of her career—and by far the biggest payday she'd ever had—was appearing in a television commercial for Tide. Still, she wasn't about to give up her dream.

That was why, when Psacharopoulos had offered her work in Williamstown, she'd come along. There were no other pressing plans for the summer. It got her out of the heat of the city, and surrounded her with theater people. The cabaret gig was fun, another string to her bow, some pin money for luxuries.

One thing she hadn't headed north in search of was a boyfriend, even if he was Christopher Reeve. But Chris wasn't about to let her slip away so easily. He sent her flowers, the typical romantic gesture, and kept inviting her out again. Finally, after ten days she gave in and agreed to see him.

The date turned out to be a moonlight swim at Margaret Lindley Pond, just outside town, which set off all manner of red lights for her.

"I thought, 'Oh God, here comes the old let's-get-naked-and-go-for-a-swim routine,'" Dana said. Chris, however, was being much more upright than that. Swimsuits were the order of the evening. "I thought that was so sweet. That night was our first kiss."

After that, they were together as much as they could be for the remainder of the summer.

"He'd come over and watch me rehearse," she'd remember later. "He'd pick wildflowers and have them carried over by an apprentice. Talk about your college romances."

It was corny and clichéd, but it worked. Dana found herself quickly succumbing to his charms, baggage and all. Very soon they were more than just an item, they were in love. He picked June 30, the day they met, as "our anniversary" (he'd done the same thing a decade earlier with Gae). Dana found that Chris was just a normal guy.

"I thought, this guy is cool. We'd do all these things that were so down-to-earth. Which is what I'm like and what I like about people. I realized he wasn't just this movie star. I found he was very much like me."

All of a sudden Chris was enjoying life again.

But one thing he did not do that summer was attend the world premiere of *Superman IV: The Quest for Peace* in London. Even without seeing what Cannon had managed to cobble together, he knew it was going to be bad, and that the reviewers would justifiably rip it apart (although *People* did note that "the first half of this film is sheer delight"—until it fell apart—and that Chris "still gives Superman a lively, engaging presence"). By staying away, he could at least try to distance himself from the disaster. Gae would have no such choice; with Matthew and Alexandra having small roles in the film—something Chris had originally arranged as a treat for his children—she was more or less compelled to attend with them.

Chris was right about the media's reactions, although it hardly took a fortune-teller to see that. They unanimously loathed it.

That was bad enough, but even worse was to come. Two men in California sued Chris, Cannon, and Warner Brothers for supposedly plagiarizing their film treatment.

"I most emphatically did not," Chris told Larry King. "I can't comment more than that."

It would be another three years before the suit finally went before the American Arbitration Association, who found in favor of the defendants. But that didn't stop the two men from pursuing it further in the courts, and losing at every step, all the way to the California Supreme Court.

It was more than infuriating for Chris. It was also expensive, at a time when he didn't have money to waste on lawyers, and it besmirched his reputation, something of which he'd always been justly proud. He'd always been a very fair man, upright in his dealings, and had he ever read the treatment and used its ideas, he would naturally have seen that the writers received full credit and compensation.

Once the Williamstown season was finished, Dana Morosini returned to New York, and Chris went with her. They continued to see each other, becoming closer and closer. Professionally, their situations were quite alike; both were looking for work. The only difference was that Chris had the bigger name. Still, it didn't seem to be helping him get roles. He was making ads (for Maidenform bras, of all things), taping audio books, how-to aviation videos, almost anything that was offered that let him sleep at night in good conscience.

And he did it all with remarkably good grace. Many actors, having tasted stardom, would have been bitter and angry at this reversal of fortunes. Instead, there seemed to be a part of Chris that was almost relieved. Now he could be a real person again, a regular guy. If it meant he had to hustle, then that was fine; he'd done it before, back when he was still unknown. His trade was actor, not star. If there was a job going in that field he could do, whether it was starring in a big-budget epic or reading a book for tape, he'd go after it, and do his best to get either one. That was what the business had always been about.

With his profile being so much lower now, he even began to think he might, finally, be able to shake off the Superman tag and be taken completely on his own terms.

For the moment he had plenty of freedom in which to think

and speculate. As fall 1987 lengthened, he was able to spend plenty of time with Dana, talking about many things. And one of the topics that came up was her moving in with him.

It was almost as if Chris was trying to repeat the pattern he'd established with Gae, as if it was a blueprint his relationships had to fit into. The fact that Gae and Dana shared some physical characteristics only heightened the impression that Dana could possibly become Gae, Mark II. In both cases there'd been the whirlwind romantic courtship, soon followed by the suggestion of cohabiting. Notably Chris didn't break tradition by immediately asking Dana to marry him.

But after some thought she did agree to move in.

They were in love, there was no doubt of that, and it was probably a logical next step, but it was hard for an observer not to notice how things seemed to be repeating themselves. She gave notice at her apartment and began packing.

But Chris and Dana decided to take a break for Thanksgiving and go up to his Williamstown house to enjoy the holiday in the country. And it was there Chris got a call asking him to be Superman again. Not for a film, not even in costume, but in spirit.

In Chile, the repressive Pinochet regime had taken power through a coup in 1973, after which they'd ridden roughshod over all manner of freedoms, particularly freedom of speech and freedom of thought. Death squads moved quite freely through the cities, towns, and villages, as the toll of the disappeared and the killed steadily rose.

Now, to make the point that the regime's control was absolute, a warning had been issued to seventy-seven actors who were given until the end of November to leave the country or face execution.

"An urgent call came out through Amnesty International

that artists were needed to go to Santiago and stand by [the artists] through the hour 'cause they weren't going to leave the country," Chris said.

The call that asked him to go came from Actors' Equity, who wanted to send a representative. Someone internationally famous as Superman—the hero who triumphed over evil and upheld all the best values of democracy—seemed like the perfect choice.

The plea touched Chris on a number of levels. More than anything, he wanted to leave the Man of Steel behind, but if he was ever going to drag the image out again, then this was the perfect reason. And as someone who'd become more politically involved, he knew he couldn't resist the request, even though it was dangerous.

With Angelica Dorfman, wife of the exiled Chilean activist Ariel Dorfman, as his interpreter, Chris flew to Santiago, joining actors from around the globe entering the country to quite literally put their lives on the line for colleagues they'd never met. The mission wasn't sanctioned by any government. They were all there as private citizens, completely without official portfolio.

Some thirty actors stayed with the people on the death squads' lists, to act as witnesses, or more hopefully, as protection. And on the thirtieth, the day those named were supposed to quit the country, they, and their foreign visitors, went to a political rally in National Stadium, where, as Chris ironically noted, "the coup had begun back in 1973."

It quickly turned into a spontaneous event, canceled by the police, only to find a new home a few blocks away, growing bigger by the minute as more and more people turned out to add their voices to the idea of freedom, in defiance of the police. It was the biggest outpouring of anti-Pinochet feeling since the coup.

Chris was asked to speak, and he did, movingly and forcefully. So many in the crowd knew his face as Superman, and here was a hero telling them how brave they were.

"[That demonstration] was the moment, as I understand it, in the Chilean political story, where people began to believe it would be possible to overthrow Pinochet," Chris said later in *A&E Monthly*. When he returned home, though, he preferred to be quite typically modest about his contribution to the proceedings. "This was not Superman to the rescue," he told the *Los Angeles Times*. "It was me as a private citizen, as an actor. . . . If you know me as Superman, fine. But we have to remember that Superman is light entertainment. This was real life. This was not just an adventure story, this was not in the comic books."

But he'd admit several years later to Elliott Forrest that "it was one of the few times I've ever been really gratified by the Superman image."

It took a great deal of bravery to go into the lions' den and stand up for an ideal he'd taken for granted all his life, to personally try and stop an evil happening to people he didn't know, and hadn't even heard of. At home he might be an actor who was spending a lot of his time looking for work, but in some places the fame he'd once enjoyed could still help bring some positive changes. Five months after the demonstration, Pinochet was out of office. That single event had galvanized the people, made them stand up and cut out the cancer in their society. Part of the responsibility for that lay with Chris, as big a feat as Superman ever managed, and all done by a mere mortal.

Although he chose to be low-key about his involvement in Chile, there were plenty of others who took note. In 1988 his work brought him two awards more valuable to him than any Oscar could ever be—a special Obie for his support of the Chilean actors, and the annual award from the Walter Briehl Human Rights Foundation.

It was only a week of his time, but perhaps the most important he'd ever spent. Being in Chile put everything else in his life into perspective. Down there actors had risked their lives every day to perform; they were people who truly did suffer for their art. Chris's career might have been on a gentle downward slope, but compared to them he had it easy; his was a life of luxury.

The start of 1988 came, and Chris and Dana settled in together, getting to know each other. The year at least began with an acting job for Chris: Not a movie, but a return to the world of the television miniseries in *The Great Escape II: The Untold Story.*

The original had become one of the classic war movies, and although this was unlikely to have the same immortality, Chris wasn't about to let the fact that it was "merely" TV affect the way he approached the role.

It was particularly important that everything he do be as good as possible, because each part was a possible calling card for another. So he was thorough, researching his character, Major John Dodge, a man who'd actually existed, interviewing his family, and coming away impressed by a man whose life, apart from escaping German prison camps, had been one long adventure—fighting in both World Wars, swimming the English Channel, and even climbing the Matterhorn. He was the man of action that Chris had always seen himself as being, prepared to take on any challenge.

"Surprisingly, I resemble him," Chris said. "He was tall, had the same hawk nose I have, and strong features. He also wore a mustache, which I wear in the film."

It was aired over a Sunday and Monday night late in the year. Like most miniseries, it wasn't about to break any records for quality, but it was nowhere near as bad as most that were aired during the average season. And, being neither particularly good nor especially bad (although Jeff Jarvis, in *People,* called it "cotton"), it simply vanished.

From Germany (actually Yugoslavia, where the filming was

cheaper, and which looked more authentic), Chris went back to working on the West Coast for the first time in a few years. In 1986 he'd had the lead in *Summer and Smoke* at Williamstown. Now he was offered the same part for a production of the play in Los Angeles. With the stage as his first love he'd have accepted anyway, but to perform it in Los Angeles, where the executives of the movie world could see him, was perfect.

In fact, it was becoming a very visible year for Chris. The play and *The Great Escape II: The Untold Story* were followed in quick succession by two television specials, *Superman's 50th Anniversary: A Celebration of the Man of Steel* (hosted, oddly enough, by Dana Carvey, when Chris was the only living actor to have played the role—a natural choice, on the surface) and *The World's Greatest Stunts: A Tribute to Hollywood Stuntmen,* which he did host.

To be fair, it was nothing remarkable, and when *Switching Channels* premiered in the theaters, there was nothing remarkable about that, either, but Chris was present, his face could be seen, people knew he was still around.

And making money, it was to be hoped, because right now he needed it. An awful lot of it. Britain's Inland Revenue had just sent him a tax demand for the kind of figure most people would imagine was an error—$1 million.

Right now, to Chris, that was the kind of nightmare he could live without. He was hardly a pauper, since he'd been well paid in the past. But at the same time, his houses and grown-ups' toys didn't come cheap. He'd established something of a champagne lifestyle. And it turned out he'd made some poor investment choices with his savings, losing a lot of what he'd hoped might leave him financially comfortable for the rest of his life.

What he needed to set things right was a big movie. But that simply wasn't happening. He'd been up for the lead in *Bonfire of the Vanities* (although, in hindsight, he was perhaps better off not being associated with that particular film), but the role went to Tom Hanks.

"I sat there and made an impassioned plea as to why it should be me," Chris railed in the *Boston Herald,* "and they said, 'You'd be absolutely perfect. I think you'd be great casting for the role and there's no way we're giving you this part.'

"What was not being said—the filling in the blanks said— was 'I'm not going with somebody who hasn't had a hit in two years.' That's the problem with [Hollywood]. It's just like stocks. Instead of being a sixty-dollar stock you're an eighteen-dollar stock."

In point of fact, it was four years since Chris had enjoyed anything that even approached a hit, with *Superman III.* But his point was real. He was no longer hot. And the only way to get hot again was to be in a big movie. But he wasn't going to be cast in a big movie unless he was hot. It was a vicious circle, and Chris was quite firmly trapped in it. The film industry was no longer about entertainment. The big studios were run not by people who thought about cinema, but by accountants. The bottom line had become the be-all and end-all of the business. As Chris would note, "Because I haven't had a hit domestically in a few years, they can't justify doing a fifteen-million-dollar movie with me."

It was galling, but unfortunately there was no escaping it. The only thing Chris could do was scare up all the work he could find from other sources to keep him going and pay off his tax debt. But there were a few compensations, like life with Dana.

"One of the things that's so great about Dana is we sail together, we dive together, we ride together. . . . We're both really good skiers," he enthused in *US.* "She plays a good game of tennis. She's a great dancer. She laughs all the time. She thinks life is to be enjoyed. So I've got a partner."

And this time, he said, there was a "very strong possibility" of marriage, a strange about-face for a man who'd been so dead set against the institution just a few years before. But he found himself able to share more with Dana than he ever had with Gae. As a person, he'd blossomed and opened with her. She was an actress; she understood the life, with its ups and downs. Gae had been a businesswoman, with heavy daily responsibilities on top of her family, a real, established life of her own that stood apart from Chris's.

When they weren't working, Chris and Dana took to spending more and more time in Williamstown. Apart from its resonances as the place they'd met, Chris loved the town, its casual atmosphere, the countryside surrounding it. It had, to all intents and purposes, become his primary residence, and as such, he became involved in town politics, helping to save the movie theater by organizing a series of screenings (including his own *Street Smart*), with the actors coming in to discuss the films shown.

"We're all doing thirty minutes of questions and answers with the audience," he explained to the *New York Times*.

He kept working. Nineteen eighty-nine brought more television, which was rapidly becoming his bread and butter, although that butter seemed to be spread rather thin when he ended up hosting specials like *Our Common Future* and *The Valvoline National Driving Test*. The highlight was a ghost story TV movie called *Things That Go Bump in the Night*.

But bills had to be paid, and that British tax debt *had* to be erased. If that was all that was on offer, then that was what Chris would take. He knew the work he was capable of, and that it was of a much higher level than this, but he didn't let pride enter into the equation. For most of his acting career he'd done remarkably well, and had been employed far more regularly than the vast majority of people in the profession.

And in the spring he'd be gainfully employed again, back onstage, in New York, working for the impresario Joseph Papp in the New York Public Theater's production of Shakespeare's *The Winter's Tale*. Although his character, Polixenes, wasn't the protagonist of the play, it was still an important role, and reunited him with one of his Juilliard classmates, Mandy Patinkin, as well as Alfre Woodward. It was the biggest thing that had happened to Chris for a while, and even if *New York's* critic wasn't especially kind to him, saying that Chris "does not so much speak his lines as gargle with them, in some sort of artfully snotty Ivy League accent," he was celebrating his return to New York theater.

The Winter's Tale is one of Shakespeare's more difficult plays, and director James Lapine made few concessions to a modern audience. The production found praise in *The New Republic,* although Robert Brustein felt that Chris's Polixenes "has a stately, aristocratic bearing, but also a muted naturalistic delivery that robs him of forthrightness and resolve." *The Nation* disliked both the production and Chris, calling him "all profile, and he delivers his lines out of the corner of his mouth with occasional flicks of the tongue for emphasis."

"The theater is my home," he said. "I've done about one hundred plays in twenty-one years. Many actors say their first love is theater, and you ask them when they were last in a play and they say, 'Ten or twelve years ago.' I do at least one, two, three plays a year."

And that was perfectly true; he'd always made time for the theater, whether at the height of his fame or at a low career ebb. It remained important to him, and now, among the TV specials, it was a lifeline of sorts, a reminder to himself of why he still loved acting so much and wanted to remain a part of it. With his credentials, Chris could quite probably have obtained a post teaching drama to college students, but being in the business, acting himself, was what he really loved. Every occasion when he became a character made even the downside worthwhile.

★ ★ ★

But *The Winter's Tale* was strictly a limited run, done in time
for Chris and Dana to go up to Williamstown for the summer, where Matthew and Alexandra would visit. Chris had cus-
tody of the children for one-third of the year, which meant,
essentially, that they spent all their school vacations with him.
Chris relished the opportunity to be with them, and they liked
Dana, which was just as well since she'd be mostly looking after
them. It certainly helped that Dana immediately also took to
Alexandra and Matthew.

"They were so darling and fantastic that when it was time
for them to visit, I'd literally drop everything. I wouldn't take
auditions. I wouldn't do jobs. Family, even before it was my
official family, was always my priority."

Once again Chris would be performing at the Williamstown
Theatre. This time it was in a new play, *John Brown's Body,*
which was set after the Civil War. The *New York Times* came
up to see how things were progressing under the new artistic
directors, Peter Hunt and Austin Pendleton (Nikos Psacharopoulos had died earlier in the year), and left saying that with this
play, the season had started "on a note of eloquence," and that
"Mr. Reeve brings great conviction to his part."

Chris was thirty-seven now. His movie career seemed effectively over, and his work in television and plays didn't fill
his time the way a three-month shoot once did. For several years
he'd had some political involvements. Now that seemed to come
more to the fore as Chris fully reached his maturity. He began
to realize that he could make more of a difference that way
than with any film he could be in.

"What I get most involved in are things like toxic waste,
recycling, water, deforestation, the greenhouse effect, and global
warming. These are important issues to me, and if there's anything I can do to help along these lines, I'll do it."

Earlier in the year, in New York, he'd worked to help stop

the development of Trump City, even meeting with Donald Trump himself, and being part of a group that suggested a compromise that pleased all the groups campaigning on the issue.

He was the narrator for the documentary *Black Tide,* which detailed the effects of the *Exxon Valdez* oil spill, and he took part in the *American Tribute to Vaclav Havel and a Celebration of Democracy in Czechoslovakia,* a fitting person to do so, since he'd been willing to face danger in the face of a dictatorship. In a prediction for the future in *US* he'd stated, "People are not going to stand dictatorships any longer. A certain level of personal freedom will be guaranteed around the world, and the global issue will not be freedom versus tyranny."

That may not have materialized as much as he'd hoped, but it wasn't for lack of effort on his part. One thing he'd seen and taken full note of was the erosion of artistic freedom at home, in the land of the free, and it worried him. The cuts in funding to the National Endowment for the Arts were motivated by politics, not economics—some politicians wanted to maintain control over government-funded artwork. It led him to wonder what he could do, and conversations with friends like Stephen Collins and Susan Sarandon brought about the formation of the Creative Coalition, dedicated to educating people in the entertainment field about political issues, and fighting for their artistic rights.

But he still had to work, since, as he told *TV Guide,* "Real life hit me in the face in the eighties." And playing Allan Pinkerton, the man who founded the Pinkerton detective agency and the Secret Service, in a television movie was about as real as work had been lately. Chris was far from sure that he was right for the part, but need dictated that he take it when offered. As television budgets went, it was more than generous, and it was a leading role, the kind of thing that wasn't coming often enough anymore.

Set during the Civil War (a period he seemed to keep coming back to lately), it was hardly high art, more rollicking entertainment, with Chris acquitting himself handily in the end. It wouldn't make him a big name again, but it wouldn't tarnish his reputation either, and he was learning that in the long run, a reputation was one of the most important things a man could have. Money couldn't buy it, but every action could affect it. And Chris's reputation was still of the highest.

It gained an even brighter sheen when he and Julie Hagerty (a woman whose movie roles only hinted at her acting ability) spent the spring on a national tour of the play *Love Letters*. Chris had taken over the role from Matthew Broderick in Boston, where it ran for several weeks. In the *Boston Globe*, Kevin Kelly compared the styles of the two men, writing that "Reeve plays it straighter. . . . [He] doesn't get as many laughs, but he is closer, I think, to the essential pathos at the heart of Gurney's script. The emotion in Christopher Reeve reading the final apostrophic letter, the tears streaming down his face . . . right now I can't imagine it without Reeve and Hagerty."

That response was typical in every city they played. They were among the most triumphal stage reviews he'd ever received, and the fact that the tour was for a good cause (Heart Strings, an AIDS organization) only improved the luster of it all.

Coming off that, he attended his twentieth class reunion at Princeton Day School, where, to his joy and surprise, he was presented with the Alumni Award for "extensive involvement in human services." And certainly it was warranted. Not only had he gone to Chile, and worked for the environment and the NEA, he'd also been involved with MADD, the American Heart Association, the American Lung Association, and many others. The name Christopher Reeve still had clout, and now it was beginning to take on resonance.

There were more TV specials, whose fees helped pay the

rent. He hosted *Night of 100 Stars III, The 16th Annual People's Choice Awards, The Earthday Birthday,* and *The World's Greatest Stunts,* but what he looked forward to was heading back to Williamstown in the summer and acting again.

With *Love Letters* he seemed to have found a new fire in himself, and it was apparent when he took the stage that summer in a revival of the old chestnut *Death Takes a Holiday,* where he starred with Maria Tucci and Blythe Danner, another Williamstown regular. Seeming somewhat surprised, the *New York Times* commented, "More than anything it is [Chris's] drollness that helps invigorate this creaky vehicle."

But great stage reviews didn't pay the bills, and television didn't offer the same paychecks as movies. The simple fact was that Chris didn't have the money to live the way he once had. So he and Dana sold the Upper West Side penthouse and moved further downtown, and he put one of his planes on the market. As answers to the financial problems went, these were little more than temporary solutions, but at least they gave them some breathing room.

Television was welcoming Chris with open arms, and there was plenty of work for him there, including a guest shot on the Canadian Broadcasting Company's *Avonlea* series. Still, if he was going to do television, the money there was in the made-for-TV movie market. The budgets were fair, the salaries were decent, and the shoots were quick. Chris had done some, but during 1990 the number seemed to escalate.

First of all it was *Death Dreams,* with Marg Helgenberger, of *China Beach* fame. It was the kind of hokum Chris hated, utterly corny and predictable, but he wasn't going to give anything less than his best, even with a clichéd script.

And then it was *Things That Go Bump in the Night.* This was a part he most certainly didn't like, in a piece about pedophilia. However, after wrestling with his conscience, he decided that in its own way it was important, and his role only took seven days to film. Before it aired, though, he was quick to offer a warning to parents in the *Washington Post.*

"I seriously hope that parents will take control of the TV set on the Sunday night that this is on. There might be some kids out there who hear I'm in the movie. They've got to explain that just because he was Superman in one movie doesn't mean he's the same in this one and they should take the time to say an actor often pretends, that it's fun to pretend, that he doesn't really do these things. . . . This is a movie for adults to watch, not for children." And, he added, his own kids would certainly not be seeing it. It was the responsible action of a father concerned for all children.

From there it was on to *Nightmare in the Daylight,* with Jaclyn Smith, the *Charlie's Angels* actress who'd become something of a mainstay on the TV movie circuit, although—perhaps because the movie was an embarrassment to all concerned—it wouldn't be aired for another year.

It all meant that he was seen by more people than at any time since his Superman days, although this time he was confined to the small screen. But it was a base, and coming off his excellent stage work the previous year, there seemed to be a new confidence and vitality about him.

Politically all the work he'd done had also helped him grow in stature. In his capacity as one of the heads of the Creative Coalition, he put himself forward to defend the National Endowment for the Arts against people who wanted to cut its funding, in the Hatch-Pell Amendment.

He traveled to Washington to offer testimony on the idea, and found himself going up against the political right, as Senator Jesse Helms and evangelist (and presidential hopeful) Pat Robertson fought hard to stop artists offensive to their morality being funded by the government.

It was an important issue, since the vote on it would delineate the boundary between politics and art, and Chris was overjoyed when the Senate finally refused to go with Helms.

"Congress decided that the NEA's critics should not be given official status as the moral guardians of America, and that politicians should not be empowered to decide what is art," he told *McCall's*. "Those decisions should be made, as they have been made for the last twenty-five years, by a panel of peers. And if an artist is found guilty of obscenity in court, he or she is asked to give the NEA back the money. . . . Politicians should *never* have the authority."

Naturally articulate, and with a presence born of many years of stage experience, Chris presented himself well at the hearings, showing an understanding of the processes in Washington and an eagerness to work for a cause he firmly believed in. The Creative Coalition, in fact, "helped introduce the concept behind the amendment that allowed a compromise to be reached," according to Chris.

It was enough to convince the head of the NEA, Jane Alexander, that Chris could have a strong political career ahead of him if he wanted it, and she urged him to run for the Senate. The Williamstown seat had just become available, following the death of Silvio Conte, who'd represented the area. But while it could have been a viable option, professional politics held little interest for Chris. Involvement in the issues that mattered to him was one thing; it was a labor of love. But to do it as a job, on a day-to-day basis, was altogether different. He knew he'd quickly lose his edge.

Besides, he had his first movie project in a few years to think about. As if someone had seen his creative fires burning a little brighter, he'd been offered a role in *Noises Off*—two roles actually, as Frederick Dallas and Philip Brent. It teamed him with Michael Caine again after a decade, Julie Hagerty, Carol Burnett, and Denholm Elliott, all under the direction of Peter Bogdanovich. He was nowhere near the head of the cast list, closer to the bottom in fact, but he was back in movies, and earning one hundred thousand dollars—which seemed like a very healthy figure to him now—for the privilege.

Based on the play by Michael Frayn, it was nothing more than a farce about a touring group of actors, but it was fun for the ensemble, and it would mark Chris's return to the big screen.

While writers generally agreed that the play was better than the film, *Newsweek* loved it, noting that it "supplies so many belly laughs it seems ill-spirited to complain. . . . No farce lover should miss it."

In his personal life things were looking up as well. Dana was pregnant, due in June 1992, and the couple decided to marry, after four years of living together.

Over dinner, "virtually at the same time we both said, 'Let's get married,' " and the words themselves turned out to be an aphrodisiac, Chris revealed. "We put down our forks and went straight to the bedroom. It was extremely erotic."

They had a small ceremony in Williamstown on April 11, with Dana seven months pregnant. Both sets of parents attended; Matthew and Alexandra were flown over for the event, and a few guests were invited.

It was a theatrical wedding, in the sense that they were both working and had no opportunity for a honeymoon. Dana was undertaking her last role before motherhood, playing in *Sight Unseen* Off-Broadway. Chris was finishing promotion for *Noises Off,* which would not do well, even with a respected cast.

Inevitably, Chris was grist for the mill for most interviewers, given the way his star had fallen, and he was the first to admit, "I haven't made intelligent choices." Elsewhere, he went into a little more detail, noting that "in the late seventies and early eighties, when I was in a position to pick and choose, I don't think I was ready for it. That can happen in this business, where the opportunity and your development don't go together, particularly if you have a big success early."

There was talk—although it would go no further than that—
of *Superman V,* and Chris let it be known that he might be
willing to play the hero one last time, if the circumstances were
right.

"If I did it, it would have to be the swan-song, the thank-
you-and-good-night. People don't want to see Superman with
a spare tire hanging over his yellow belt."

Chris was thirty-nine now, and perhaps too old to offer
America Superman's kind of action. Lines had begun to form
on his face, and whereas his looks had occasionally seemed callow when he was young, now he'd fully grown into his face.
And, it seemed, into his life.

CHAPTER TWELVE

Will Reeve came into the world on June 7, 1992, in Williamstown, Massachusetts, the place Chris and Dana had more or less made their home.

The parents had joked about naming him Murray, after the Murray Hill section of Manhattan where a sonogram had revealed the child's sex, but Will it was going to be.

This time there would be no transatlantic parenting. The couple would have a nanny, but there'd be no shuttling around the globe for this kid. Chris and Dana finally sold their apartment in the city and bought a farmhouse in Westchester County, not far from Dana's parents.

"We love New York," Chris said of their decision, "but we didn't want to raise our child in the city. It was time to move. We like our privacy."

Along with his new parenthood, Chris seemed to have really found his feet again, after several years in the wilderness, and he was beginning to undergo something of a professional renaissance. He'd never be a major star again, he realized that. But he was also happier with it. The pressure was off. He could get on with his life and enjoy himself. Work was coming in thick and fast, with any number of television specials, ranging from the self-help *Mending Hearts* to *What's Cookin'?*

And the TV movies kept on coming, too. He was Father Thomas Cusack, torn between the sanctity of the confessional and the need to stop a murderer in the rather doubtful *Mortal Sins* (which, bad as it was, still outclassed the dreadful *Monsignor*), and Humphrey Van Weyden in an adaptation of Jack London's *The Sea Wolf.* Neither was likely to bring him awards, but it was work, pushing his name out there again and keeping him afloat.

Shortly after Will was born, Chris undertook his yearly appearance at the Williamstown Theatre Festival, playing Nandor, the lead in a revival of *The Guardsman.* This time, however, would mark his last time performing there. Much as he loved it, under the regime of the new artistic directors things had changed in a way that didn't suit him, and it was time to let it all go. Just from the festival; not from the town—it seemed unlikely he'd ever really leave that—but from the annual round.

Williamstown's theater festival had been good to him. It was a place he could always find excellent work, and more importantly, the place where he'd met Dana. But all good things must come to an end.

As soon as the run was over, he went happily back to the grind of making movies. The watershed that had threatened to sink his career had passed, and now there was a small cinematic demand for his services again, in the type of strong character roles that played to his strengths. *Morning Glory* had him cast opposite Deborah Raffin, in a script she'd help write from LaVyrie Spencer's book. He was cast as an ex-con during the depression trying to establish a new life, working on Raffin's farm, only to find himself the prime suspect when a woman in town is murdered. It wasn't challenging drama; in the end it proved to be little more than lightweight entertainment. But

Chris still ensured that his performance was solid. Over the years he'd become something of an acting craftsman, a person who could work with any kind of role. Sometimes there'd be inspiration, and he'd turn in something incandescent, but for the most part now he was proving himself to be solid and honest, with a weight lent by years.

Filmed on a small budget, *Morning Glory* was one of those independent releases that are destined to see only limited release on the art house circuit. But that was still enough for *Newsday* to offer a reassessment of Chris:

"This movie isn't big enough to make Reeve a star again. But the impression he makes here is good enough to suggest that a reversal of perception—and fortune—won't be long in coming."

Indeed, it already had. Chris wanted to act, and projects were beginning to come his way. And just after he finished filming *Morning Glory,* an offer arrived that would offer him new artistic respect—the part of Lewis in *The Remains of the Day,* the new film from Merchant-Ivory.

It was a definite move back up the ladder. In the past ten years the Merchant-Ivory team had gone from strength to strength, and the Oscar that was about to come for *Howards End* would mean they'd finally be classed among the big producers. And they'd done it all while keeping to very strict budgets, without sacrificing the quality of their films to try to appeal to fickle commercial markets. They made the films they wanted to make, the way they wanted to make them. Being asked to act for them was an honor, as Chris knew only too well. It served to negate any image forming that he'd become just another TV face, another Robert Urich.

The Remains of the Day was a curious story, centered around the life and relationship—or nonrelationship, really—of a butler (Anthony Hopkins) and the housekeeper (Emma Thompson) in an English country house. Chris played Congressman Lewis, an American guest at a country estate in the 1930s, who returns as its new owner in the 1950s.

It wasn't a heroic part, not a major role, or even pivotal in the movie. But the whole piece had depth and gravity, to match its marvelous acting, and it put Chris in very fine company indeed. As he noted, it was "nice to be able to play characters with some mileage behind them. That's more rewarding." But he'd entered his forties now; he had plenty of mileage of his own behind him now. The days when he could play an ingenue or an action hero were long since gone.

It was the first time in many years that Chris had been involved in anything this lavish. He had nothing but respect for the other talents involved, most especially Emma Thompson, an actress who, as he said, could easily produce "Great Moments." Unusual and unlikely as the story was for American audiences (essentially *Upstairs Downstairs* with a very psychological twist and remove), it proved popular.

And it was rewarded with eight Academy Award nominations. Even though it didn't win in any category, a virtually impossible task against *Schindler's List* and *The Piano* that year, it remained a cinematic highlight. And chief among its fans was Chris himself, a member of the supporting cast.

"I don't regard that as my movie—I was a visitor—but it's the best movie I've ever been in. Anthony Hopkins gave one of the best performances ever captured on film."

For Chris, whose Lewis represented the New World politically and symbolically in the film, standing as the lone voice not espousing fascism in the 1930s dinner party for a visiting Nazi official, it offered a political prelude to his activities in 1992, working for the Clinton-Gore ticket in the presidential election.

"I've watched in despair as every environmental law is trashed by [the Bush] administration and Quayle's Council on Competitiveness," he said in anger.

He had the ear of Al Gore, himself very concerned with the environment, and toured some of the most polluted sites in the Northeast with him.

After his run-ins with Republican politicians who wanted to exercise their own form of censorship over the arts, and the desecration of the environment to aid industrial corporations under Bush (and before him, Reagan), it was natural that Chris would gravitate toward lending his support, time, and name to the Democrats. He was concerned not just with the world he lived in, but the one that Matthew, Alexandra, and now Will would eventually inherit. So when the Democrats achieved victory that November, with Clinton taking over the White House, Chris was naturally jubilant, trusting that the shift in the winds would mean more liberality in Washington, and a much tougher stand on environmental issues.

Indeed, for him, work seemed to be involving politics in one form or another during much of the next year, 1993. There was the release of *The Remains of the Day,* with its political subtext; a television special, *Earth and the American Dream,* devoted to ecology; and a Larry King presentation of *November 22, 1963: Where Were You?,* a recollection of John F. Kennedy's assassination on its thirtieth anniversary.

Most important was his involvement in what had originally seemed like a local censorship issue. It had been taken up by the press and made into something of a cause célèbre. In Tucson, Arizona, a high school drama teacher had been fired from her job after letting her class perform a scene from *The Shadow Box,* a play which had won both Pulitzer and Tony Awards when on Broadway.

Its subject was cancer and death, but underneath it offered a vague theme of homosexuality, which was ample to offend a number of parents, who demanded that the play be banned by the school. Under that kind of pressure, it was, and then the teacher, Carole Marlowe, was ordered by the principal to go through all the plays in the school's drama library and censor—quite literally black out—every "objectionable" word.

She did that, even though to many people such bowdlerization seemed ridiculous. But when she let her class—at their request—perform a scene from *The Shadow Box* during the school's Fine Arts Week, the authorities gave her no choice but to resign.

The students demonstrated in her support, making the incident national news. At that point the Creative Coalition became involved. Chris flew to Tucson and made a speech, appearing as part of a panel of actors defending Marlowe and her actions. Then, that same evening, the impromptu troupe gave a reading of *The Shadow Box* to a packed theater (notably the citizens of Tucson didn't stay away in droves). Joining him were Creative Coalition cochair Blair Brown, Estelle Parsons, Michael Tucker, and others—all very well known and respected names in the business. None of it managed to help Marlowe retain her job, but in a show of solidarity, her colleagues throughout Arizona nominated her for the state's Teacher of the Year award.

While it wasn't anything like a complete triumph for the Coalition, they had at least done all they could, and awareness had been raised. Perhaps, next time, the parents and the principal might think before overreacting.

Chris's career continued to hum along at a steady pace. The momentum that had begun over the last couple of years continued with back-to-back movie offers.

First there was a comedy, *Speechless,* somewhat freely based on the romance of Mary Matalin and James Carville, who'd worked on opposite sides of the political fence as spin doctors during the '92 election, before marrying each other.

With stars like Michael Keaton and Geena Davis, neither of whom was a massive draw, it was never going to be a major film, but it was typical of the workaday projects that filled Chris's calendar. The script was perfectly likable, funny and charming in parts, with Chris as usual heading up the supporting cast, playing a very egotistical television reporter who was engaged to Davis's character.

The work, and the knowledge that for most of the next year he'd be based in Los Angeles, made Chris and Dana decide to temporarily relocate there, rather than have him commute between coasts in his free time. It kept the family together, and that, above all, was what Chris and Dana wanted—no separations. So they rented a house in the Hollywood Hills and settled in for the duration.

One item of trivia that the papers were quick to pick up on with *Speechless* was the fact that it contained both the big-screen Batman and Superman in the same movie. By now, though, Chris was quite adamant that his superhero days were a thing of the past. Whatever discussions there had been for a *Superman V* had come to naught, and if they were revived, they would no longer include him. He had, he said, been the "custodian" of the role for a while, but "if they do it again, there should be a new custodian for this generation."

Speechless, when it appeared in theaters, turned out to be exactly what it had looked like—a small, pleasant comedy, soundly and capably acted. Chris performed well as the reporter who'd been everywhere and done everything, and found himself singled out for praise in the *New York Times.*

"The story's sidelines are especially enlivened by Christopher Reeve," Janet Maslin wrote, while critic Gary Arnold went one step further, noting that "Mr. Reeve has quietly evolved into a versatile character actor. . . . It's only a matter of time before he's 'officially' rediscovered and celebrated, like John Travolta in *Pulp Fiction.*"

And indeed there were some parallels in the careers of Chris and Travolta. Both had been big stars at the same time, only to fade from the limelight. Unlike Chris, though, Travolta had kept active in movies, even having some hits with the *Look Who's Talking* series, even if no one seemed to take him that seriously. But *Pulp Fiction* saw his real rehabilitation as an actor and a star, after which he returned to the ascendant.

In some ways, he'd been luckier than Chris. But they were very different actors. Travolta had come out of television. For Chris, stage work lay at the heart of his performances. That was where he kept returning to center and replenish his artistic self. He was content to be working regularly, as part of the ensemble, finding the level that seemed to suit him best.

The other film on his agenda was a remake of *Village of the Damned* under the direction of John Carpenter, which appeared with an R rating. The original, in 1960, had been based on John Wyndham's novel, *The Midwich Cuckoos,* and had spawned a sequel, *The Children of the Damned.*

This version didn't exactly set the world alight. Quite the opposite; in fact, it quickly disappeared into welcome obscurity. And as Dr. Chafee, acting alongside Kirstie Alley, Linda Kozlowski, and Mark Hamill—all once big names like Chris— he could have been forgiven for thinking he'd wandered back into some acting twilight zone himself.

Still, it was work, and a movie, and he wasn't about to turn it down. Every little thing was a job to be savored and done as well as possible.

During 1994, he'd return to the stage again, for what would turn out to be the last two occasions, although no one could have foretold that. In March he was briefly in New York, as the narrator for a single revival performance of Stephen Sondheim's *Allegro* at City Center; then in the summer he went back to the Williamstown Theatre Festival, with which he'd had such strong associations, to help them celebrate their fortieth anniversary. He and Julie Hagerty performed *Love Letters,* which had done so well a few years before, and he read a scene from *John Brown's Body,* in which he'd starred at Williamstown in 1989.

From there he moved into an extremely busy time. He worked on a trilogy of westerns for CBS, which would eventually air under the title of *Black Fox.* He did all his own riding, often several days at a time for the shots, and, said director Robert Halmi Sr., "He was so in control. He did all his own stunts."

There was a job as narrator for a 4-H Club video designed to prevent head injury while riding. He did a similar public-service announcement for the American Equestrian Association, posing for a helmet-safety poster.

He was set to take part in Francis Ford Coppola's remake of *Kidnapped,* with his scenes due to be filmed in Ireland in June 1995, and negotiations were also under way for Chris to direct his first feature. It really did seem as if he was on the rise again.

But television movies had become his real bread and butter, pieces like *Black Fox,* or the movie he now contracted to make for HBO, *Above Suspicion.* In the last few years, dramas made for cable had come a long way. They had an artistic edge free from network constraints, and their quality was often as good as anything the cinema could offer. So when the opportunity to stay in L.A. and take the lead in one of these movies came, it was a chance to be grabbed, particularly when the part seemed so meaty and challenging. As Officer Dempsey, he had to portray a police officer wounded in the course of duty, a man who was paralyzed and confined to a wheelchair, even contemplating suicide at one point, and suspecting that his wife and brother might be having an affair.

It was such an eerie irony. This was the last movie Chris

would make before his accident, and the last to be screened. His work was excellent, as good and luminous a performance as he'd ever given on-screen. His research had even taken him to a spinal-cord trauma unit, where he'd seen the effects of paraplegia and quadriplegia. With chilling prescience, he commented to *Hard Copy*, "You see how easily [spinal injury] can happen. You think, God, it could happen to anybody."

As 1995 began, Chris was a contented man. He was growing older gracefully. He might have lost the lead in *Jefferson in Paris* to Nick Nolte, but there was still plenty on his plate. There were other jobs waiting, he had his family, and there was his political involvement. He'd become a well-rounded individual, happy with his lot in life.

And as one of the heads of the Creative Coalition, he found himself back in Washington, fighting for the National Endowment for the Arts again. This time the battle was more or less to the death, however, as a Republican Congress wanted to eliminate the NEA. It was more than just a financial move, since the NEA was viewed by the right as a symbol of all that was wrong with America—liberal, arty, and immoral.

Along with other actors, Chris appeared at the National Endowment for the Arts Advocacy Day, an attempt to rally support which might halt the actions of Congress, speaking to the crowd in a measured way, coming out in favor of deficit reduction, but pointing out that there was no reason to "fear the arts."

In the event, they were successful. The NEA remained, but with its funding cut 40 percent. It was, the Coalition thought, "a moral victory."

By the end of May Chris was ready for a vacation. He'd been riding for a few years, and owned horses. There was a chance to take part in a show at Commonwealth Park, Virginia, over Memorial Day. It would make a perfect getaway for himself, Dana, and Will. Located close to the Blue Ridge Mountains, they could explore and relax, and Chris could ride the tension out of his system. He might not win anything—he hadn't yet advanced to the level where he was likely to be a serious competitor—but he relished the idea of a challenge.

It all sounded perfect.

CHAPTER THIRTEEN

Looking forward to the long weekend, Chris, Dana, and Will flew down to Virginia in his plane and checked into the Culpepper Holiday Inn. He was ready to ride on his newest horse, Eastern Express, which he'd purchased in California earlier in the year.

Chris had taken up riding a few years before, and had soon begun to compete as a show jumper. He was under no illusions that riding was an easy sport.

"Horse jumping is the most dangerous thing I do," he'd told the Associated Press, and for a man who enjoyed flying, gliding, skiing, and scuba diving, that was quite a statement. He'd been thrown three years earlier, while competing in Canada, but had sustained no injuries.

The event he was about to participate in was the spring horse trials of the Commonwealth Dressage and Combined Training Association, one of the more prestigious on the amateur circuit. It would be a three-day meet, covering all facets of horsemanship, and held at the Commonwealth Park equestrian grounds, which covered some two hundred acres of ground in the shadow of the Blue Ridge Mountains, well away from the hustle and bustle of the cities. Chris would be one of three hundred competitors, all eager to prove themselves and their horses.

He'd been down in the area before, looking for Thoroughbreds he could buy. That was how he'd originally come to hear of the trials, another opportunity to push himself and his mount against both obstacles and time. In some respects he hadn't changed from the young man who got his thrills learning to fly some twenty years earlier. If there was a challenge that stretched his body and his mind, he relished it. But at the same time, he took every sensible precaution, wearing both a protective vest and a helmet.

Chris even had his own colors, the blue and silver of his alma mater, Princeton Day School. He comported himself like a professional, but in fact he'd just moved up from the novice category. He'd won one event, in Vermont, a year before, then placed third in the New England novice championships. With his height and weight, it was unlikely he'd ever make the first rank—he was simply too big—but he was still determined to advance as far as he could.

In Commonwealth Park he was up against some very good riders, people who were able to devote more time and money to it than was possible for him. Even so, at the end of the first day, he was acquitting himself well.

After the dressage stage on Friday, May 26, he found himself in the middle of the pack, a very encouraging result. Dressage was the real test of discipline and communication between horse and rider, with the mount required to perform set, intricate steps on command. To work well, man and creature needed to be quite empathetic with each other. That he'd done so well on Eastern Express, a horse he hadn't had much chance to work with, was quite an achievement, especially since he was up against so much experience.

What he was relishing, though, was Saturday, which would see the cross-country jumping phase. The course consisted of fifteen fences set through several miles of the park, with the emphasis on clearing each obstacle cleanly, riding against the clock. It was demanding, both mentally and physically, for all the participants.

And on Sunday, with that out of the way, the final part of the horse trials would be the show jumping, the highlight for many, and for those who'd arrive to watch, perhaps the most familiar of all the different events.

On a cross-country course, every jump has to be approached differently. Judging them to perfection is both an art and a skill, creating exactly the right momentum, the perfect speed and balance to clear, land cleanly, and gallop on. There is no room for any lapse of concentration when a rider has to think not only of himself, but of a half ton of animal between his legs. The horse has to trust its rider implicitly, and immediately obey even the most subtle command.

Chris set out, and easily cleared the first two fences, riding well, making good time, and pushing Eastern Express. This was their chance to move up in the field and end up in a good position for the final day's show jumping.

He came in for the third fence, nothing particularly difficult, just three feet high and made of wooden rails set in a zigzag.

"The horse was coming into the fence beautifully," Lisa Reid told *People*. She was an experienced trainer who knew how to judge horses and riders. "The rhythm was fine and Chris was fine, and they were going at a good pace. The horse put his front feet over the fence, but his hind feet never left the ground. Chris is such a big man. He was going forward, his head over the top of the horse's head. He had committed his upper body to the jump. But the horse—whether it chickened out or felt Chris's weight over its head, I don't know. But the horse decided, 'I can't do this.' And it backed off the jump."

Chris, his center of gravity so far forward, was unable to stop. The horse halted, but he kept on moving, pitching out of the saddle and over the horse's head. It seemed to onlookers as if he banged his head on the fence before his forehead hit the ground, and he lay sprawling, completely motionless.

Later, Chris would only be able to recall that his hands had somehow become tangled in the bridle.

"The bridle came off, and my hands were tied up in it, and I couldn't break my fall. Otherwise, it would just have been a sprained wrist."

A medical crew was immediately called, but the first person on the scene was Helmut Boehme, who'd organized the weekend of trials.

"He was unconscious when I got there. He was not moving. He was not breathing."

The first task was to resuscitate Chris, and the medics did just that, pumping air into him to keep him alive on the journey to Culpeper Hospital. As soon as he arrived it became obvious that he was severely injured, and was going to need specialized spine treatment. A quick decision was taken to fly him to the University of Virginia Medical Center in Charlottesville, some forty-five miles away. They had the capability to deal with Chris's injury.

Within an hour of the fall he was in Charlottesville, transferred by helicopter, and being evaluated in the emergency room.

Dana had been called—she and Will hadn't gone to the cross-country event—and as she drove from the Holiday Inn in Culpeper the doctors tried to assess the full extent of Chris's injury. Certainly the signs weren't good. He was still unable to breathe without help, and he hadn't yet regained consciousness.

Word had traveled quickly that it was Christopher Reeve who'd been injured. Someone had alerted the press, and the news that he'd been hospitalized had already gone out on the wire. Reporters from all over the globe were taking the next available flights to Washington, preparing to drive south. In his career Chris hadn't returned to the big time. Now, as a victim, all the newspapers wanted to know about him.

Dana was able to sit with Chris, who was still unresponsive. Will was being looked after by the nurses; Dana didn't want him to see his father that way, to have that image imprinted on his mind. She'd called Chris's parents and his brother, Ben, who were all making arrangements to travel down. Barbara Johnson had called Gae Exton, who'd gathered Matthew and Alexandra, both teenagers now, and had taken the first transatlantic flight to Dulles Airport.

She and Dana had never met before, but this was no time for rivalries or comparisons.

The hospital released a preliminary statement about Chris as the first of the media people arrived. It seemed to say a lot, but remained typically vague, noting only he was in "serious but stable" condition, and that he had "a cervical injury and is under close observation."

But the real truth was that the doctors didn't know much more than that yet.

Reporters continued to flood into the facility, trying to get more information, wanting to see family members, to have anything at all to write beyond the bare-bones press release. But they couldn't have what didn't exist, and the last thing anyone in the family wanted was to face the media.

Chris finally regained consciousness after four long days, and that was a first step; there was no coma. But he couldn't breathe on his own, and he still couldn't move. He was paralyzed.

When he came to, Barbara Johnson told NPR, "he was confused" and "mouthing but not speaking words. . . . He was asking what had happened. It was tough. You could see him struggling."

It was more than tough for Chris, and it was a waking nightmare for those around him. They were being hounded by the press, who were also questioning doctors and nurses, anyone they could find. Chris's press agent in Los Angeles knew no more than they did, possibly even less, since her information was coming at second hand from Dana and Chris's parents, and there was nothing they wanted released yet because, until the tests were complete, no one could really know how grave the situation was. The only thing that was immediately apparent was that Chris wasn't about to get up and walk anytime soon.

It would be Wednesday, May 31, before Dr. John Jane, the neurosurgeon in charge of the case, would be able or willing to offer more information, saying that Chris might require surgery to stabilize his upper spine, and that any speculation about Chris's long-term condition was "premature."

That made it all sound relatively straightforward, but the reality was much grimmer. As one member of the hospital staff put it bluntly, "They are praying for a miracle."

The following day Dr. Jane elaborated on the injury, pointing out that Chris had "no movement or spontaneous respiration." He'd sustained a fracture of both the first and second cervical vertebrae—almost the worst place to receive a spinal column injury, even though, thankfully, the cord had not been severed, which was what the doctors had initially feared. Had that happened, his chances of survival would have been slim at best. Even now his life still largely hung in the balance, and he'd developed pneumonia in one lung, a condition which didn't especially worry Dr. Jane, pneumonia being common in these cases.

"He's alert but cannot make sounds because a breathing tube has been inserted into his windpipe. . . . He cannot control his expiration, so what he has to do is to say words in an exaggerated fashion and use local breaths to make a sound, and it doesn't work badly. It's not good for back-and-forth rapid conversation, but it's good enough to communicate."

Once he did come to, it didn't take long for Chris to realize just how grave his situation was.

"Dana and I were alone in the hospital room. . . . The doctors were saying I might not pull through. I remember saying to Dana that maybe it wasn't worth the trouble, maybe we should just let me go. If Dana had looked at the floor or taken a pause, it would have been difficult because I would have thought, 'She's just being noble.' But without missing a beat, she looked me right in the eye and said, 'But you're still you and I love you.' And that saved my life right there. That put an end to any thought of giving up. Then my three kids came in. . . . And I asked myself, 'How can I possibly leave them?' "

"I could see how much they needed me and wanted me," he explained to Barbara Walters later, "and how lucky we all are that my brain is on straight. The thought [of dying] vanished and has never come back."

Not that the dark times didn't come crowding in on him as he lay in the hospital bed.

"The demons would get me in the middle of the night. In my dreams I'd be whole, riding my horse, playing with my family. . . . We'd be making love, we'd be doing everything. And then suddenly I'd wake up and it's two in the morning and I'm lying in bed and I can't move and I'm on a ventilator. . . . Those are the worst times."

As terrible as Chris's injury was, with the spinal cord not cut there was still a chance of recovery. Essentially, he had a break in the nerves of his spinal cord, "like the bridge is out," he'd say later. But the best odds the doctors were willing to give for his survival were fifty-fifty. Most immediately, once the pneumonia had gone, he needed an operation to fuse the fractured vertebrae and stabilize his head and neck.

By June 5 he was in good enough condition to be wheeled into the operating theater and given into the hands of Dr. Jane.

"We have a ninety percent success rate," Jane announced beforehand, "and if it fails, we'll simply try again. The mortality rate is four percent."

It would be a while until they knew if it had worked. If it did, Chris would be able to sit upright again, and his chances of making a recovery might improve. He might even be able to move a little. But the dark reality was that it looked unlikely that he'd ever manage to walk again.

The surgery, which normally took five hours, extended slowly to seven, the minutes ticking by. The C-1, or top vertebra, had been shattered, and every minuscule bone fragment had to be found and cleaned out before other bone from Chris's hip could be placed between the two vertebrae, and then everything was fused together with titanium wire, which was finally attached to the head, using microscopic holes drilled in the skull.

The good news was that the phrenic nerves remained intact, so the spinal cord definitely hadn't been severed. The damage had mainly been on the left side of the cord. So in theory Chris should regain some feeling, and, said a hospital spokesperson, "The phrenic nerves, which travel through the neck and chest to the diaphragm, are indeed not disturbed, indicating that the paralyzed actor has the mechanism to breathe on his own."

When and if that might happen remained to be seen, however.

The outpouring of good wishes was huge. The president and Mrs. Clinton sent their wishes, as did people in Hollywood and New York's theater community, Chris's political friends, and most of all, ordinary people from all over the world, who only knew him through his movie and television work. On June 9, Dana Morosini issued a statement to thank everyone—the hospital, doctors, nurses, but most especially the well-wishers.

"Most of [Chris's] day is spent listening to messages from well-wishers," she said. "I can't begin to express how important these are to him. . . . He is a fighter and survivor of the first order. But this has to be the toughest challenge he has ever faced. I know it is mine. Chris needs all the positive support he can get right now and that is why he and I are so deeply grateful for the outpouring of love and concern we have received from all over the world since the accident."

Chris's spirits, she told the assembled journalists, were mostly good. "He has been visiting daily with the children and other family, watching hockey on TV. . . . He has already begun the first stages of physical and occupational therapy."

For the first time since the fall, he was able to be in a semi-upright position, and he could eat some solid food. Air still had to be drawn into his lungs with a respirator, but he could exhale on his own.

Within a week of the operation, Chris told the doctors he had feeling in his chest, and he was able to flex the trapezius muscles in his back. Dr. Jane was pleased with his patient's progress.

"That's a positive sign. He is consciously moving this part of his body."

His neck still needed to be supported in a firm brace, but when the respirator was removed Chris was able to speak. He could be pushed out into the sun in a wheelchair. Things were still far from good—just how much so was brought home to him when Will celebrated his third birthday at the hospital and all Chris could do was sit by, unable to participate, or even hug his son—but they were already beginning to get better. Dark as it all seemed sometimes, at least he was alive. The news that he was going to be a quadriplegic—unable to move either his arms or legs—didn't come as a shock. He'd already been able to figure that out for himself. But that didn't mean he had to accept the idea that he'd remain that way.

His spirits had been lifted by the visit of an old friend. When a man wearing scrubs, a mask, and a surgical cap entered the room, Chris assumed it was yet another doctor who'd come to take a look at him. Even the Russian accent didn't seem too strange, until the man said,

"I'm goink to haff to, just go down, hold on. . . ."

At that point Chris realized who it was, "and his eyes lit up, and he started to laugh."

It was another turning point, the return of humor.

"I had a fifty–fifty chance to live," Chris recalled. "I was hanging upside down [in a hospital bed], and I looked and saw a blue scrub hat and yellow gown and beard and heard this Russian accent. There was Robin Williams being some insane Russian doctor. I laughed and I knew I was going to be all right."

Robin Williams was one of Chris's oldest friends, from their days together at Juilliard. They'd become stars at the same time, but whereas Chris had slowly had to settle for a lower level of fame, Williams had moved on from being television's Mork to all manner of film roles, showing the full versatility of his range, dramatic and comedic, along the way. But the two had never lost touch; Chris was the godfather of one of Williams's children. Together they'd gone out and raised hell on a couple of occasions, and now Williams was here to do anything possible to cheer up his friend.

Chris had to think completely of himself, of getting stronger, and Dana had to consider virtually everything else. With little more that the hospital could do for him, once he'd fully recovered from the operation Chris would be able to leave Charlottesville, and he'd be needing to spend many months in a rehabilitation facility, one which specialized in treating upper-spinal-cord injuries. It was the next step in the recovery process. There were several recommended by the National Spinal Cord Injury Association, an organization that Chris would soon come to know intimately.

The two that seemed most promising were in New York and New Jersey. All the immediate family members lived in that area (Barbara Johnson in Princeton, New Jersey, Franklin Reeve in Connecticut, brother Ben in Martha's Vineyard), which would make visiting, something they all considered a priority, that much easier. Of the two, Dana finally decided on the Kessler Institute for Rehabilitation in West Orange, New Jersey. It was away from the bustle of the city, but still readily accessible.

The date set for his departure was June 28. It had been an eventful month, one which had seen him stare at death and come back. The family organized everything. Already they'd begun to lobby for more money to be pumped into spinal-cord injury research. The day before Chris left the hospital, his brother was in Washington, testifying on the matter before a Senate committee. With typical Reeve thoroughness he'd researched the matter extensively, as Chris soon would himself, becoming an expert on the matter.

On June 28 Chris began his journey to West Orange. It was a tricky journey, involving more than simply moving an immobile patient. A nurse had to manually pump air into his lungs during the entire trip. A private plane picked him up at the Charlottesville airport and flew him to New Jersey, where he was transferred to an ambulance with a police escort for the short drive to the Kessler Institute, where he was finally settled, exhausted, Dana and Will by his side.

The future wasn't going to be easy. The first, and most difficult, step had been taken, but a whole journey still lay ahead, one that would find him redefining and testing every single one of his limits. The months he'd spend in Kessler would also be expensive. At two thousand dollars a day, the cap on his insurance, which had once seemed so high, would soon seem remarkably small.

Chris, quite simply, had a simple long-term goal: He was going to walk again. Nothing was going to deter him from that, and as far as he was concerned, the purpose of his time at Kessler wasn't to help him adjust to his new life, but to enable him to achieve what he ultimately wanted.

Initially he was restricted to his bed or a wheelchair, seeing his physician, Dr. Marcalee Sipski, every day, along with physical, speech, occupational, and respiratory therapists, all of whom worked in concert with Chris to help him overcome, or at least do all he could with, his new disability.

From the very beginning his days were highly structured. There was a breakfast of fruit at 7 A.M.—solids were making up a good portion of his diet now—followed by an hour of physical therapy, with exercises designed to strengthen the muscles in the neck and shoulders, and the therapist moving his arms and legs to prevent atrophy.

After that came occupational therapy with lessons in how to operate his new Quickie P300 electric wheelchair, a massive forty-thousand-dollar investment, which he moved by sipping or puffing air through a tube, after which came speech therapy. Or else he'd spend time on the Regis cycle, which would automatically move his legs, exercising them, and giving his entire body an aerobic workout.

In the afternoon, Dana and Chris, often accompanied by others from the family, would come and push him through the grounds.

"Christopher is very motivated and extremely sensitive to what's going on," Dr. Sipski commented shortly after he arrived. "When the doctors or therapists give him a task, you know he's going to make sure he does it perfectly. If there's an obstacle to overcome, he's going to overcome it." At the same time, she had to admit that "I am not very optimistic" about Chris ever regaining any further muscle movement.

Dr. Craig Alexander, who was Kessler's head of psychology, was also spending time with Chris, and after two weeks there described him as "a passionate, intelligent and confident man who strives to direct and control as much of his treatment as possible. He believes there is a purpose for everything including his present battle with disability."

And a battle was exactly how Chris saw it, one that he could win. He was putting his competitive nature to work, this time fighting nature.

"As a kid, I was always competitive," Chris recalled, "and I've always responded well to a challenge. If someone says, 'You've got to try twenty repetitions of this exercise,' that gives me the incentive to do thirty or thirty-five. You have to push."

And throughout his time at Kessler, Chris was determined to push as much as possible. After only two weeks he was on a tilt table in the physical therapy room, turned semiupright, his first experience at anything like standing. It was used to pump up his blood pressure, which was low, given the fact that he couldn't move. Dr. Sipski, who'd been used to seeing him either in bed or his chair, walked in.

"For the first time I had to look up," she said. "He's really tall and has these piercing blue eyes. He looked like what I was used to seeing in the movies."

Chris began to refer to Sipski as "Coach," and that was largely what she was, encouraging him in all his efforts. She wanted him to succeed, but knew that a dose of reality had to be injected into his possibly futile dreams.

"An injury like his impacts every system of the body. There are so many potential complications. It can take years to adjust." At the same time, her job was to ensure the patients left Kessler able to function at their highest possible level, ready for whatever might come. She knew that before his accident, Chris had been hired to direct a film, a job that was still waiting, whenever he was ready to undertake it. It still seemed feasible. "I still expect him to direct a movie," Spiski said. "I don't see any barriers in his way."

For himself, Chris wasn't about to acknowledge that they even existed.

"Chris spends much of his day conducting his own brand of therapy," Dana Morosini told reporters. He worked as much as he could for the causes he'd always supported, as hard as before the accident, and spent time with family and friends, including Robin Williams, always his manic self, who'd become a frequent visitor.

"He is achieving things that are astonishing," Williams said, enough to show him, he felt, "the sheer force of the soul."

One thing the staff believed possible was to enable Chris to breathe without a respirator. For many months they'd worked toward it, but it was seeming like a hopeless task. He could blow air out easily enough, but he had difficulty taking enough in.

"My doctors . . . had basically given up on my breathing without a respirator. But in November I said, 'I want to try this again.' They came to my room and I tried taking ten breaths. I averaged 80 cc of air per breath, which wouldn't keep a parakeet alive. The next day, my motivation was very strong, and I was able to average 450 cc per breath. The doctors were stunned."

The next day Chris was up to 560 cc. The following day he announced to the physicians that he wanted to try breathing without the respirator.

"I breathed seven minutes," Chris said proudly. "After that, it built up rapidly. I just did it. . . . I'm not going to be chained to this respirator for the rest of my life."

It was a remarkable feat, but typical of his determination. Having set himself a goal, he would do everything he could to achieve it, no matter how long it took. But there were setbacks. He experienced bad bedsores from lying prone for so long, and on one occasion a new medication sent him into anaphylactic shock, causing a worrying overnight stay in a local hospital.

Every single day Dana and Will were there to see him, spending as much time with him as they could. Chris was their priority. They both had a great deal to learn about caring for him. Eventually he'd be coming home, sooner rather than later, they hoped, and Dana would bear the brunt of his daily needs. They had a nurse living in, but even so, both she and Chris knew it wasn't going to be easy for either of them. What they had to rely on to help them through was their love for each other and for Will.

"Our relationship has been fantastic since we first got together," Chris told *Ladies Home Journal*. "But I would say this is our highest level. . . . We're more focused on what really matters—the family and how far love can take you. How far commitment can take you, to help you through something like this. We draw strength from each other."

And strength was exactly what Dana needed. Not only was she at Kessler each day, she also had to arrange for modifications of their Westchester County house. Ramps needed to be built to give him access, doors widened, any manner of things to make his life easier. The only thing that couldn't be managed was an elevator to the second floor. Other than that, it would be ready whenever he was.

Friends came to visit. Colleagues from the Creative Coalition, people he'd worked with in theater, television, and film, all came to see him. For some it seemed a strange and unnerving experience, finding Chris this way.

"I sense them throwing glances around, being uncomfortable and uncertain. But within moments, I can see them relax. I have found no one who looks at me with pity. Any anxiety, fear, or awkwardness fades away almost immediately."

His life and his horizons improved vastly when he received a computer that would work on voice recognition. The new software, Dragon Dictate, obeyed his commands, and let him communicate with the world outside his room by fax and E-mail. He could work on the Internet, and "I can talk to my two older kids in England, where they go to school. I ask them how their day was, and play chess with Matthew."

It opened a door, and got him thinking beyond his immediate physical recovery. Even confined to a wheelchair for the present, there was no reason to stop doing things. Once he was strong enough there was still that movie to direct, and he could continue with his political activism. Now he had a new and much more personal cause, lobbying the government on behalf of all spinal-cord injury victims. With his name and stature, he would at least be listened to. He was, after all, a man who could get the ear of the president.

He'd done his research, and knew that $5 billion was spent each year just to keep people with spinal-cord injuries alive. If that amount were applied to research, he believed, results would quickly be forthcoming, which would end the large long-term drain of dollars on Medicaid and Medicare.

"Two hundred thousand people in the United States alone have the same problem as me," he explained, "and a lot of them are very poor people. A lot of them are on welfare. . . . I'll bet you, in my life, and maybe in the next ten, fifteen years, if the public will demand that the politicians spend that little bit of money, and make that investment, I'll be up and walking around again."

It was the first salvo in what would become his ongoing campaign. He wasn't going to spend his life in a wheelchair, and he was determined that no one else should have to, either.

Every day brought a step forward of some sort or another for Chris. Sometimes it was a mental victory, being able to speak out. Other times it was more tangible and physical, like regaining some feeling in his left leg, or occasional twinges in his spine. Every little thing helped him believe there was a very real future for him, something he'd doubted when he'd first woken up in the University of Virginia Medical Center to learn he was a quadriplegic.

Since the end of May all his time had been spent in either a hospital or an institution. The farthest he'd gone was around the grounds, and during the summer even that activity had been limited, because paralysis meant his sweat glands couldn't function, causing the danger of him literally overheating.

Soon enough, he knew, he'd be moved again, back home, and he was eager to be there. But before that he needed a trial run in the outside world, and October 16, 1995, provided the perfect occasion. The Creative Coalition, of which Chris remained cochair, was having its annual Spotlight Award Dinner, and Robin Williams would be the honoree.

The event was being held in New York, less than an hour's drive from Kessler, close enough to be comfortable, particularly with a therapist in constant attendance.

None of the audience was told in advance of Chris's appearance; only the organizers knew. In case of some mishap, forcing him to cancel, it was better to keep everything secret. The meal over, the five hundred guests at the Hotel Pierre settled down for the ceremony. What they saw was Chris being wheeled onstage and up to the microphone.

As one, the audience stood and clapped. The ovation went on for five full minutes. Few had ever expected to see Chris appear in public again, and certainly no one had thought it would be so soon.

"I never knew how much love was pointed in my direction," Chris told them. "Since my accident I think I've heard from every one of you. I want to thank you from the bottom of my heart. You've helped me turn my life around."

He reminisced about Williams visiting him in Charlottesville, and Williams responded by announcing, "I came that day, and I'll be back a million times. This man is my family. He's the godfather of my son!"

It was an emotional, intense occasion, but Chris couldn't allow it to pass without planting a thought in the minds of the people listening to him. It was another short speech, a seed to get all these influential people—names like Robert F. Kennedy

Jr., Barbara Walters, Susan Sarandon, and Tim Robbins—to help him work for more research into spinal-cord injuries.

"Somebody's got to take that leap," he said. "Somebody's got to stand on the edge of the Grand Canyon and say that with a good enough running start we can jump this thing and cure spinal-cord and other neurological problems."

It wasn't a case of lobbying in the faint hope that it might cause a miracle cure. Chris firmly and truly believed it was possible, that with a push and some government help it could all happen.

By the end of November Chris had reached the point where he was able to breathe unaided for more than eleven minutes at a time. The Kessler Institute had done virtually all it could for him. Any greater recovery, if it happened, would come with time and work. Although he still took some nourishment through a tube, the doctors believed he was about ready to eat solid food for all his meals. It was time to think about moving on, to start rebuilding his life outside the four walls.

The date for his homecoming was set for Wednesday, December 13. Six and a half months had passed since he'd fallen off Eastern Express in the horse trials. His life had changed in more ways than he could ever have imagined. Now it was time to really begin looking to the future.

CHAPTER FOURTEEN

The first time I pulled up the driveway, I had a moment when the tears let loose. There was a Rip Van Winkle effect. I had been away for so long, and there I was, home again, but under very different circumstances. I couldn't walk up the steps. But day by day, you get used to it. You say, 'Wait a minute. So I've got a ramp. It's not the end of the world.' "

Coming home, strange as it seemed at first, was a huge boost to Chris's morale. Being out of Kessler, marvelous as the place had been for him, really made him feel like he was on the road to recovery, and his spirits soared. Not only his, but Dana's and Will's, too. With his father at home again, Will could finally relax. During Chris's first days in the hospital, Will had kept riding a broom, and falling off, in his own attempt to understand what had happened. Maybe Chris couldn't play the way he once had, but his fears of dad never coming back were all banished. In fact, Chris said, "Now he uses me as a jungle gym. He climbs on me all the time."

At first, the doctors felt it might take Chris some time to adjust to his surroundings, that he might even be depressed, being in his house again and not being able to do the things he once had. In fact, it had the opposite effect. Not only was he emotionally happier, but his blood count, blood pressure, protein count, and oxygen levels had risen, and he was able to breathe for fully fifteen minutes without the respirator.

Already he was busy, more determined than ever that nothing was going to slow him down. In Kessler he'd given his first interview, to Barbara Walters for ABC's *20/20* program.

Walters had requested an interview not long after the accident, and never received a reply. Eventually, though, Dana called, "saying he was going to do an interview and that he had decided to do it with me," Walters said. "And I really didn't believe it."

She spent three days with the couple, and announced later, "I think this interview had a greater effect than anything that I have done in all the years at ABC, because there are not that many times when you come across that extraordinary true, shining love that Chris and his wife have for each other."

Another thing that impressed her was "the message that you are your mind, you are your intelligence."

"She made us feel unself-conscious," Chris noted. "And that allowed the television audience to see two people as they really are. . . . Barbara gave us room to . . . talk about how much joy, hopefulness, laughter, and love remain in our life."

She was so moved that she made a Christmas donation to the American Paralysis Association in honor of Chris, and in her Christmas card, urged others to do the same.

While not strong enough to attend himself, Chris sent a video copy of the interview to the hearings of the Senate committee in charge of appropriations for the National Institutes of Health. At that point, a cut in research funding seemed likely, but after viewing the tape, the politicians relented and actually increased the funding, another victory.

Chris was taking on as much as he could, accepting a prestigious nomination to the board of the American Paralysis Association. He'd also been contacted by Joan Irvine Smith, a

California philanthropist and ardent equestrian. She'd followed everything that had happened to Chris since his accident. What truly moved her was the fact that Chris bore no rancor toward Eastern Express. The horse had been sold, but that was simply a matter of expediency and finances; Chris still loved horses.

What she proposed to Chris was a Reeve-Irvine Research Center, to be based at the University of California, Irvine branch (known as UCI). It would, a press release stated, "support the study of trauma to the spinal cord and diseases affecting it, with an emphasis on the development of therapies to promote the recovery and repair of neurological function."

Smith, through her Joan Irvine Smith and Athalie R. Clarke Foundation, was willing to donate $1 million to fund the center if UCI could raise another $2 million. But even there she was willing to help, donating the proceeds of the Oak Falls Classic, a top-flight equestrian event held annually in San Juan Capistrano, California, to the fund. And at the September event she'd host the awarding of the Christopher Reeve Research Medal.

"The courage and perseverance Christopher and his wife Dana have shown over the last several months are truly extraordinary," Smith said when the center was announced on January 10, 1996, "and I'm honored to do what I can to help him and the thousands of other individuals suffering from spinal-cord injuries."

With Chris's friends in the entertainment industry, the money UCI needed—and even more—was quickly forthcoming, to make the dream a reality.

And during January Chris took another big step, forming the Christopher Reeve Foundation. The idea had been brewing during his time in hospitals. Research needed all the financial support it could get, from any and every source. There were things the government couldn't give money to, but a more private fund might be able to help.

People wanted to help, that much had been clear from the massive outpouring of sympathy he'd received. A charitable foundation would give them a way to offer tangible help, to know that any money they contributed would go to the right places. It was something he felt might make a difference. And there was more: While much of the money raised was given to research, Dana coordinated other funds to be used for advocacy for the disabled, and equipment and home care for those who couldn't afford it alone.

While he spent a lot of his time looking at the outside world and the future, Chris also needed to focus on himself and the here and now. Being home was exactly what he needed mentally, but physically he needed constant attention if all the progress he'd made in Kessler wasn't going to come to nothing.

He had to undergo breathing exercises two or three times a day, and his lung power was rapidly increasing. From fifteen minutes just after arriving back in his Westchester County house, he'd zoomed up to ninety minutes at one stretch without the respirator, even if he did still need it when he was speaking. His legs were exercised with a StimMaster cycle, which offered electrical stimuli to the muscles in his legs, as well as other electrical stimulation to the leg muscles. And finally there was the tilt table, which he'd been using for months.

Obviously, Chris couldn't do all this himself, and while Dana did everything she could for him, she was physically unable to move a two-hundred-pound man from one piece of equipment to another. A nurse lived with the family to give assistance, and be on hand in case of any small emergency. Chris's personal assistant came in every day, too, to work with him on business and fund-raising matters.

One matter nagged at both Chris and Dana day and night, however. All the therapy was expensive, totaling some $400,000 a year, with a cap of $1.2 million. Even then, he knew he was

luckier than the millions of Americans who had no health insurance at all.

"It's terrifying," Dana admitted. "At this rate, our insurance
will run out in three years. And since Chris has a preexisting
condition he won't be able to get more insurance."

However, it seemed that a financial savior was at hand. A
London paper, the *Daily Star,* reported that Robin Williams
had told Chris he would cover all his medical costs once his
insurance ran out (although other sources would later refute
this story). Supposedly the two had made a pact while still at
Juilliard that whoever made it big first would help the other. If
it was true—and there was little doubt that Williams could easily afford the amount, given that his net worth was in the re-
gion of $100 million—then it was something of a godsend to
Chris and Dana, one huge worry lifted from their shoulders.

Were it not true, however, they'd have plenty of problems,
as Chris told the *Washington Post.*

"A year or two ago we seemed to be well off. Now my
picture has changed. And there are so many people whose po-
sitions are even worse."

He began lobbying hard to raise the insurance cap to $10 mil-
lion, writing to every senator, and in fact, Vermont Republican
James Jeffords, who was Chris's friend, actually attached an amendment to a health-reform bill with just such a provision.

Immediately there was opposition from the powerful insurance companies, even though Chris was able to cite a study
showing that the higher cap would cost just an extra eight dollars a year in expenses to consumers on their insurance. It was
something he believed in fighting tooth and nail on, recording
a radio spot that played almost constantly in Washington, urging people to support the amendment. *USA Today* weighed in
on his side in an editorial. But in spite of all the efforts, the
Jeffords amendment sank in the Senate, outvoted 52–46.

It was as if, now that he was home, Chris was determined to make up for his lost months. He pushed himself physically and mentally with political work, and even ventured out to the circus with Will. Perhaps it was inevitable that he'd encounter a few setbacks.

The first came on January 16, just a few weeks after he'd returned to the house. He had to be rushed to Northern Westchester Hospital Center, suffering from autonomic dysreflexia, which had resulted from a urinary infection. His blood pressure had soared dangerously high, and although it was quickly stabilized, he was still kept as a patient for a few days for observation.

Home again, he still refused to take it easy, although he admitted that "I feel weak and tired at the moment." He concentrated on increasing the time he could remain off the respirator, breathing through his nose, managing up to thirty-five minutes. It was, he said, "like walking up a steep hill. It was a nice success for me. Whenever I have a setback, I demand more of myself. . . . I look for ways to challenge myself so that when I'm up and going again, I won't have lost my approach to life. If you give up once, you could become one of those people who sit and stare out the window."

Obviously, Chris wasn't about to let that happen; indeed, the whole prospect seemed to terrify him, but he was someone who'd always been active, both mentally and physically. He needed to fight against the whole idea of becoming a burden, a dead weight.

By early February he could feel that real progress was being made. In a sitting position, he could regularly breathe off the respirator for ninety minutes at a time. Tests showed that 75 percent of the sensation is his left leg had returned, and there was a marked increase in his shoulder movements. It was as if, very, very slowly, his body was healing itself. How much further it would go, no one knew, but he would keep pushing it for all he was worth.

And the opportunities were coming in for him to push it a long way. There was a rather sad irony in the fact that Chris's accident had returned him to the kind of celebrity he hadn't known since the beginning of the 1980s. He'd been in magazines and on television, and the offers were still coming in, far more than he could feasibly handle. Warner Brothers was planning a major animated feature, and was interested in him providing one of the voices. Studios were pleased to suggest directing jobs.

And there were any number of speaking engagements. Chris's courage, his refusal to meekly accept what fate had handed him, had landed him quite rightly in the inspirational category. Soon he was a part of that circuit, making up to fifty thousand dollars for a single appearance. Maybe it wasn't what he got into acting to do, but he would be the first to admit that he needed money, and other big-cash parts wouldn't be forthcoming anytime soon.

In the meantime he organized a benefit for the American Paralysis Association, to be held at Radio City Music Hall in New York on March 22. Anything that occupied his time was welcome, and when it was an event like this, supporting *his* cause, he was pleased to use his clout to get things organized.

His first foray into public speaking came in March, when he traveled to Green Springs, Ohio, where he was set to open an $18 million wing of St. Francis Health Care Center, the facility to specialize in the treatment of spinal-cord patients. Going any distance was arduous, particularly on a plane, but he needed to get used to it; he'd be doing plenty of it in the months and years to come.

In fact, another trip was planned for just two weeks after, this one a little longer, taking him all the way to the West Coast. Chris had been invited to the Sixty-eighth Annual Academy Awards, to be held on March 25. Perhaps the organizers were surprised when he accepted, but he knew this was a chance to appear in front of the most powerful people in Hollywood and raise his voice for better roles for the disabled. Not only would they be listening, but literally all over the world people would be tuned in to the show. The old Chris wouldn't have missed such an opportunity, and the new Chris wasn't about to let it slip by, either. However, when he received the invitation, in January, and agreed to appear, "I put the phone down and said, 'What have I done?' "

Transporting him was almost like a military operation in its intricacy. The logistics were coordinated by Neil Stutzer, who was president of Access of New Jersey, a company which arranged travel for the disabled. For Chris to attend the Oscars, Warner Brothers had supplied one of their corporate jets, which helped, but even so there were plenty of problems to be overcome. Chris had to fly in a prone position, which meant the wheelchair was little more than baggage. There were backups and precautions for any and every medical emergency that might happen in flight, all written in a seventy-five-page manual that Stutzer had prepared himself—he even came along to make sure everything went smoothly. And Chris needed to be attended, not only by Dana, but also a doctor and nurse. Whether in a van or a plane, every bump sent him into spasms. The ventilator had to remain connected; his blood pressure had to be constantly monitored for spikes. It wasn't so much a journey as an ordeal.

Word of his attendance at the Oscars was kept secret. Beyond the organizers, only a very few people knew he was in Los Angeles. He and Dana checked into the Beverly Hilton on March 23 under assumed names, staying in the Presidential Suite. Staff security even cleared the halls as they went to their room so no other guests would see him. After dinner with Robin Williams and his wife, there was a quiet evening with some friends from the profession, including Emma Thompson, with whom Chris had worked in *The Remains of the Day.*

The theme he planned to address was "Hollywood Tackles the Issues," and his sole insistence was that a clip of *Coming Home,* the film that starred Jon Voight as a wheelchair-bound Vietnam veteran, be shown as part of the video montage. He cowrote his own speech with producer Susan Winton.

It was a big night, a major event, both for the awards and for Chris. The Creative Coalition dinner five months before had been one thing, but that seemed like an almost informal gathering compared to this.

Early in the evening, radio stations managed to leak the news that he'd be at the Dorothy Chandler Pavilion, but it didn't matter; by that time most of the guests had already arrived.

Everything seemed to have been perfectly stage-managed, but there were a few inevitable last-minute glitches. Just twenty minutes before he was due onstage Chris informed Quincy Jones that he didn't want the orchestra to play the theme from Superman as he entered.

But music was hardly needed; the mere fact of his appearance would be dramatic enough in itself.

It was timed as the virtual climax of an evening which had seen its share of emotion, as Kirk Douglas, recovering from a stroke and unable to speak properly, received a lifetime achievement award from his sons, and Gerda Weissmann Klein recounted in chillingly matter-of-fact fashion her memories as a Jew during the Holocaust.

Chris was the crescendo of all that. Directing his wheelchair by sucking and blowing on the straw, he rolled onto the stage. As they had at the Creative Coalition, the audience stood as one, applauding. Chris was one of them, a man who, to all intents and purposes, had come back from the dead, and they were happy to celebrate his return.

"What you probably don't know is that I left New York

last September and I just arrived here this morning," Chris joked
as the ovation finally died down. "And I'm glad I did because
I wouldn't have missed this kind of welcome for the world."

"I saw so many warm and accepting faces," he said later.
"It felt like a homecoming."

And everyone, those there in person and the billion people tuned in around the globe, listened raptly as he introduced
brief clips from *Norma Rae, Thelma and Louise, Platoon, Philadelphia,* and *Coming Home.*

He pointed out that the film industry had the ability to make
these kind of films and have them seen by millions of people.

"Hollywood needs to do more," he said in conclusion. "Let's
continue to take risks. Let's tackle the issues. In many ways our
film community can do it better than anyone else. There is no
challenge, artistic or otherwise, that we can't meet."

Later, the event over and emotions calming, he and Dana
went to the Governor's Ball to celebrate what had been another little—or in this case, big—victory.

"I can't tell you how much his presence lifted everybody,"
said producer Susan Winton, and Scott Henderson, Chris's agent,
pointed out that "Chris loved showing people that he's back."

And back he definitely was. Speaking engagements were fine,
and now he needed an immediate involvement in political issues for the disabled, but he still wanted to be involved in movies
and theater. They were his lifeblood, the way he'd earned his living for more than two decades. It was one of the ways he de-
fined himself, and to lose that part altogether would have been
very hard.

But Chris wasn't the only one with artistic dreams; Dana, too,
had had a career, one she'd put on hold to care for Chris.
Not that she ever resented it; he was her husband, her priority.
But she also had a need to act, to be able to have that outlet.

She and Chris had shared many details of their private life

with the media, including the fact that they could make love, even if it was a "spontaneous reaction" on Chris's part, rather than anything they could control. Through all the interviews, Chris had lauded his wife, and the reporters had been happy to follow that angle.

"She makes jokes about the media portraying her as 'St. Dana,' " a friend said. "But she doesn't want to be that. She says, 'I am just a woman whose husband fell off a horse, and I'm going to take care of him. That's what you do.' "

Now she had a chance to return to work, though, and Chris wasn't about to stand in her way. The New Jersey Shakespeare Festival was producing *The Two Gentlemen of Verona* and Dana had been offered the role of Julia. It was close enough to home that she could commute, and Chris had his nurses and attendants in the house.

In truth, by now she probably needed a chance to break free, if only for a few hours a day. For virtually a year she'd spent almost every waking hour with Chris, going through some very difficult times without much in the way of light relief.

And as Chris organized his life, he was doing more and more. Why shouldn't she? This was more of a return to the normality they both wanted, and that they'd known before.

In fact, Chris's diary was becoming quite full. On April 18 he was scheduled to be in Atlanta to speak at the "Success '96" seminar, and he would return to the city in August to be the master of ceremonies for the Paraplegic Games, whose eleven days would be televised—by CBS, no less. He'd put his name on the dotted line for a multimillion-dollar deal with Random House to write his autobiography, collaborating with writer Roger Rosenblatt.

And on April 1 he finally signed to be the voice of King Arthur in an upcoming Warner Brothers animation, *The Quest for Camelot*.

As gratifying as all his political activism was, this was perhaps the most important step he'd taken since his accident. He was working again.

"Chris Reeve is a wonderful actor whose talents we all admire tremendously," said Max Howard, the president of Warner Brothers Feature Animation. "He was our unanimous first choice for the role of King Arthur, and we began negotiating his participation quite a while ago, when the character was beginning to take shape. Chris's voice will infuse the qualities of energy, power and warmth into King Arthur, whose presence is an important component of our story. We're thrilled that he's joining this project."

The plan was for Chris to record his dialogue in New York during the summer, as his schedule allowed. He'd be working alone, as the other principal voices hadn't yet been cast.

It was, in essence, an extended voice-over, but it was work nonetheless. And with these floodgates opening, there was more coming through.

Before his accident Chris had signed with Ryser Entertainment to direct a romantic comedy, and that seemed likely to happen before year's end.

Keith Samples, the head of Ryser, was definitely looking forward to it.

"Chris is incredibly focused, and he has a strong sense of moviemaking," he said. "Obviously the locations will have to be very carefully thought out. Chris gets fatigued, and I don't think you want to put him in a situation where he is shooting fourteen hour days. But I don't think we'll have to."

Chris also agreed to work on a project that struck much closer to home, narrating an HBO documentary, *Without Pity: A Film About Abilities,* which according to the press release "profiles Americans with a variety of disabilities who seek independence as well as access to society."

Then, in May came a prospect he could really sink his teeth into. HBO, eager to follow up on the idea of Chris directing a film, had requested a meeting with him.

Fred Zollo and Bonnie Timmerman, two producers, along with Will Scheffer, a scriptwriter, and some executives of HBO NYC, an offshoot of the cable giant, drove up to Westchester County to see Chris at home.

He'd already been sent the script for *In the Gloaming,* a drama dealing with a young man suffering from AIDS who returns to his parents' house to die.

Chris liked the idea, but he wasn't as thrilled with the execution.

"I said, 'I'm gonna open with a couple of comments that may get me fired here,' " he remembered in *Entertainment Weekly.* "I told them [the script] had potential, but it also had problems. It read like a play. . . . [So] I said: 'Basic changes need to be made. If you think it's too much, by all means get somebody else. I'd be wrong for the movie.' "

On the surface it sounded like a very brash move. After all, Chris had long expressed the desire to direct, but had never done anything more than second-unit work. Laying down conditions long before filming was scheduled, before a contract had even been signed, seemed very arrogant.

But one thing Christopher Reeve has never been is a fool. He realized full well that now his name had cachet, and the idea of Christopher Reeve, the quadriplegic, directing a film about AIDS had great publicity value for HBO. His name would bring in many viewers who wouldn't otherwise watch it. HBO wanted him as much as he wanted to direct, and that put him in a very powerful position, where he could make statements that would seem outrageous coming from most novice directors.

Of course, Chris didn't say what he did simply as a power play. He was a professional. He'd been in the business long enough to know when a script worked and when it didn't. If he was going to put his name on this piece, he wanted it to be the very best it could be, from beginning to end.

In the Gloaming had been adapted by Scheffer from a story by Alice Elliott Dark which had appeared in *The New Yorker.* However, in Chris's view, it had "too many words."

Having received a promise of a full rewrite, the group then began to talk about casting. HBO wanted big names, people like Gene Hackman, up-and-comer Leonardo DiCaprio, or Johnny Depp. Chris had other ideas, actors who in general weren't such household names, but nonetheless superb.

"It's part of [HBO's] process," Chris said later. "If you came in with *Ordinary People,* they'd have ideas. But that's what helps you discover what you really want. I call them 'over my dead body' moments."

In the end he did win. Robert Sean Leonard was the son, David Strathairn the father. The only really major name was Glenn Close, who agreed to play the mother.

"I was in the middle of a twelve-week shoot in Australia when Chris faxed me," she recalled. "The last thing I was thinking of was to work again."

For her, one of the deciding factors—apart from working with Chris—was that a location in Pound Ridge, New York, close to Chris's house, had been quickly settled on, and Close lived nearby.

The other big plus was that she'd known and respected Chris for fifteen years and "really wanted to be with him in his first directing attempt."

Robert Sean Leonard, from a different generation and not personally close to Chris, was more sanguine about things.

"I'm always skeptical of first-time directors," he said, "because the job's much harder than people think."

At the same time, he had to admit that Chris came into the project with a strong reputation as a craftsman, someone who wouldn't take on a job he couldn't complete—and complete well.

Shooting was set for the fall, giving everyone plenty of time to prepare.

For Chris, however, it stood as a prelude to a remarkably busy summer. His first trip was to Washington, where he was once again lobbying for more money to be spent on research for spinal-cord injuries.

"We know him as Superman, flying through the air," said Senator Arlen Specter after his appearance. "To see him come in, propped up in a wheelchair, is really heartbreaking."

But when it came to pushing Congress to spend more money on something that would directly affect his own future, Chris didn't mind playing the Superman card if it helped.

His stature and previous activism certainly helped get him an appointment with President Clinton, who promised $10 million in new funding. Given the total federal budget, it was little more than a raindrop in an ocean, but every amount, no matter how small, counted. And in the Senate, Specter was willing to try to have that amount increased to $40 million, a slightly larger raindrop.

Given the way that research was advancing, this really was a case where throwing money at a problem could solve it. As Chris worked the names in Washington, *Science* published an article from researchers at the Karolinska Institute in Sweden, who'd severed the spinal cords of rats, then transplanted nerves from other parts of the body. The new nerves had regenerated and produced enough of a recovery for the rats to walk.

That was a massive breakthrough, but only one of many going on around the globe, particularly in the United States. Steroids were being experimented with, a substance called 4-AP had proved hopeful in clinical trials, and the Salk Institute was experimenting with gene splicing.

Everything offered hope, although scientists had come to the conclusion that there wouldn't be one single cure, as had long been thought, but that a series of remedies working in concert might end up working miracles.

For Chris, and the hundreds of thousands like him who wanted to walk again, it was all good news. But Chris had one more immediate ambition in particular. On his fiftieth birthday, in 2002, he wanted to stand unaided and raise a toast to the family who'd supported him so much. The way everything was progressing, it didn't seem unreasonable at all.

In the meantime, he was doing everything in his power to help generate the money that could bring it about. He kept playing the political game in Washington, and he wrote about the funding problem in *Good Housekeeping,* urging readers to write if they supported increased funding (an article which resulted in Specter's office receiving some twenty-five thousand letters).

His work had been so excellent, his visibility and profile so high, that the American Paralysis Association was pleased to elect him chairman of its board of directors.

And even the American Medical Association gave him a special award for his work to try and remove caps on medical insurance.

But most importantly, Chris was asked to address the Democratic National Convention in August. Since his accident he'd shown himself to be such a symbol of courage, refusing to give in to his disability, that he'd become a symbol of bravery in America.

At least, he had to most people. But there was a vocal minority among the disabled who objected to the stance he was taking. To them, the idea of searching for a "cure" implied that they were sick, which they wouldn't accept. They regarded themselves purely as differently abled.

Cyndi Jones, who published *Mainstream,* a magazine which

campaigned for rights for the disabled, said that she was "in favor of research that makes a difference in the lives of people with disabilities as they live them." That meant not only access to buildings, and housing designed for them, but "bowel and bladder function—there's all kinds of stuff they could put a little bit of money into."

By placing himself at the forefront of research for a cure to spinal-cord injuries, Chris incurred their wrath, and raised the dust of controversy. In a way, this minority had a point. People ended up in wheelchairs for any number of different reasons, such as multiple sclerosis or strokes, which weren't going to be really addressed by the research Chris was advocating. For them, research into the things that would make life easier *was* needed. But it was impossible to address everyone's problems. Some had chosen to resign themselves to life lived in a wheelchair, and Chris was unwilling to do that. He was fighting it every inch of the way.

It was sad, then, that in his refusal to buckle under, he found himself opposed by groups like Incurable but Able to Vote, a group which opposed him as a spokesperson for the disabled. They planned a demonstration at the Democratic National Convention in Chicago, stating that instead of spending money on a cure that might or might not happen, the dollars would be much better spent enforcing the Americans with Disabilities Act. They even demanded another disabled speaker at the convention to address the need for civil rights.

This was America; they had their rights of protest and dissension. But it was Chris who, more than anyone, had made people around the country aware of the problems of the disabled. In television interviews by Barbara Walters, Larry King, and Katie Couric, the public learned of the daily tribulations, the seemingly mundane things like pressure sores and lack of bladder control that those in wheelchairs have to live with all the time. More than that, they'd seen how in less than a minute the man who'd flown across their screens could become a quadriplegic, down to earth with a bang.

And the fact that he was determined to overcome his limitations, to break through the bonds that had been placed on him by nature, made him a wonderful role model, someone who had, quite literally, turned into a superman.

Having him as the opening-night speaker for the Democratic National Convention on August 26, 1996, showed just how much of a symbol he'd become.

"We use his personal example in trying to overcome a debilitating injury, and having a community rally around him, and the inspiration he has given to others in struggling to overcome his injury," was the assessment of David Eichenbaum, who was the communications director for the Democratic National Committee, which had issued the speaking invitation.

But to others, most particularly the Republicans, the choice of Christopher Reeve simply highlighted the perception that the Democrats were more about personalities—more specifically, show-business personalities—than politics, which was strongly denied by Kiki Moore, in charge of communications for the convention.

"If anybody believes that because Christopher Reeve makes a living in the entertainment field, that takes away from his real-life experience, then they are probably missing an opportunity to learn some valuable lessons," she responded.

And so, on a steamy August night in Chicago, Chris directed his wheelchair onto the convention podium. By now the sustained applause had become a standard response to his appearance. This, however, was the most important address of the many he'd delivered in the last few months. Televised live across the country, it gave him a chance not only to make his pitch for more funding, but also to give a message to America.

He began by touching on the issue of family values, so heavily touted by the Republicans in 1992.

"I think it means we're all family, and we all have value," Chris said. "And if that's true, if America really is a family, then we have to recognize that many of our family are hurting."

To blunt the swords of groups like Incurable but Able to Vote, he praised the Americans with Disabilities Act, saying it "must be honored everywhere. . . . Its purpose is to give the disabled access not only to buildings, but to every opportunity in society."

The truly important thing, though, in Chris's mind was to work for a cure.

"When we put our minds to a problem, we can usually find solutions. But our scientists can do more." He pointed out that nationally the government spent $8.7 billion on the disabled through various programs. "But we spend only $40 million a year on research that would actually improve the quality of their lives, get them off public assistance, or even cure them. We've got to be smarter, do better."

He cited the example of Franklin Delano Roosevelt, the former president who'd put the New Deal into place in the 1930s, and himself a man who'd spent much of his life in a wheelchair because of childhood polio. When FDR had dedicated the new buildings for the National Institutes of Health, before the Second World War, he'd said that "the defense this nation seeks, involves a great deal more than building airplanes, ships, guns, and bombs. We cannot be a strong nation unless we are a healthy nation."

In conclusion, Chris said, "America is stronger when it takes care of all of us. Giving new life to that ideal is the challenge before us tonight."

It was, as he'd intended it to be, directed at the hearts and consciences of a nation. All across the political spectrum there were stirrings to cut back funding wherever possible, and Chris wanted to remind the politicians of their duties and responsibilities to look after the country's citizens.

His years as an actor helped, but what really made Chris into such an inspirational speaker was passion. The political had become extremely personal, and every time he spoke he was quite literally fighting for his future. He could breathe without the respirator, but he couldn't speak without using it, making every word doubly important.

In the end, of course, Clinton handily regained the White House, but while the Democrats had a president, they didn't have control of either the House or the Senate, which meant that at best the Democrats could only hope for compromise, and often failure.

Chris was eager to make his directorial debut. He'd waited years for the opportunity to come his way, dropping hints, and now he was more than ready. All the preparations had been made, and his anticipation was rising at the thought of the challenge. Before filming began on *In the Gloaming* in late September, though, he had two important engagements in Canada, the first to start the fund-raiser for the Toronto Hospital and the Hospital for Sick Children. Their goal was to raise $12 million for neuroscience research, and who better to kick it all off than Chris.

By now he'd become the figurehead, the poster boy of the cause. But reality ran a great deal deeper than that. Yes, the public knew his face and was shocked by the tragedy of it all—which he would readily admit was no worse than anybody else's in a wheelchair—but at the same time, he *was* willing to get out there, to speak, lobby, to do anything he could. Perhaps his motives weren't always altruistic, since he himself would benefit from research breakthroughs, but that gave him an even greater stake.

More than anyone in sixty years, since FDR, perhaps more

than anyone at all, he'd raised public awareness of people in wheelchairs, and most particularly of spinal-cord injuries and their effects.

And that, of course, was why Toronto wanted him. His schedule had become so busy that they'd been forced to contact him six months ahead of time. Even then it hadn't been easy. As with his other appearances away from the New York area, the logistics became complicated. There was only one small jet, the Challenger, that would let him sit in his chair for the entire trip, and still be able to accommodate his nurses and attendants. That meant the Toronto organizers had to scurry round, finding someone with such an airplane who was willing to loan it for a good cause. They did, and everything went according to plan—something that had to be a constant worry. Chris was growing stronger all the time, but he also lived on a very delicate edge, and he drove himself as hard, probably harder, than he ever had. Certainly a chair hadn't slowed him down.

After Toronto he pressed on to Montreal, to address the Congress of Neurological Surgeons. While not a physician or a scientist, Chris had become very familiar with what was going on in neurological research, the key that held the potential to get him out of the chair and back on his feet again. Often researchers contacted him directly to tell him of their results.

This time, however, Chris played his other big card, talking again of the need for an increase on the lifetime insurance cap, noting that a "million dollars might seem like a lot of money, but if you have a catastrophic injury, it goes very fast." And for once he was talking to sympathetic ears, since the CNS had also come out in vocal support on the issue.

And from there it was back to New York, and a final few days of much-needed rest before the filming began. His body, obviously, didn't have the strength it once had, and he needed to be alert for the month of shooting ahead. Everything else was important, too, but this could be the beginning of a new career. He needed to be focused the entire time.

As with anything else in his life now, directing a movie meant dealing with certain constraints. Chris couldn't actually be on the set, since the constant hiss of his respirator would bleed into the sound recordings. So he was forced to undertake his directing duties from a nearby room, out of sight, watching everything on monitors and listening through headphones, communicating with the cast and crew via a microphone, which led to his nickname on the production of "His Omniscience."

He'd thought long and hard about the differences between acting and directing, and had developed a strong understanding of both.

"Acting is such a direct reward," he told *Entertainment Weekly.* "You're the center of attention. . . . When you're directing, you're using the other side of your brain, the side that's analytical, that makes decisions. So this injury has really forced me to shift gears."

The cast, which had finally been rounded out by Whoopi Goldberg and Bridget Fonda, had all agreed to work for far less than their normal fees as a favor to Chris. So now he had a full quotient of excellent names at his disposal, a script that achieved the effects he desired, and hopefully the time and budget to do what he needed. The pressure was on. Now all Chris had to do was deliver.

For someone who spent his days tucked away from the set, he was very much in charge of everything, knowing what was going on everywhere, and taking full responsibility for the production.

"To have someone on your set who cannot move, but who's in charge, is a rather incredible thing," marveled Robert Sean Leonard. "Most first-time directors have a hard time with the chaos that goes on. [They tend to] put lots of the decisions on the cinematographer's shoulders. Not Chris. He held his own. . . . He was the anchor."

What he wanted was something he'd achieved often in theater, but not really in film or television—for the cast to work together like a family, to become a family to each other—and since they were playing a family, that was doubly necessary. He was on the actors' side. He knew exactly what it was like for them.

But it was draining for him, there was no doubt of that, and he had to ration his energy, as the shoot was only one part of his job. After that there remained all the postproduction work, the editing and the final cut.

For part of the movie Leonard, playing Danny, a young man dying of AIDS, had to be in a wheelchair, and Leonard did have to wonder if Chris found himself overempathizing with Danny.

"At times, I thought Chris might have connected [with] Danny a little too much," he mused. "When you know you're going to die in six weeks, like Danny, it's not the same as knowing you won't walk or move your arms again. They're both shocking, life-changing things to face. But they're very different things."

What he really hadn't taken into account, though, was the time, just after his accident, when Chris only had a fifty-fifty chance of living. He *had* been there, he did know, and so his relation with the character was perfectly normal. And Bridget Fonda offered a different viewpoint to Leonard's when she said, "[Chris] was always a daredevil physically. Now he's an emotional daredevil."

The filming completed, on time and within budget, always two big stresses for a director, new or otherwise, Chris allowed himself a few days before beginning the postproduction work. But even that wasn't a rest, or not completely. He attended the opening night of the National Horse Show in Madison Square Garden.

At a preshow fund-raiser (which would benefit both the

American Paralysis Association and the Reeve-Irvine Research Center), Chris was to be honored for his work.

It was a fitting backdrop. In spite of everything that had happened, Chris had never lost his love of horses, or of watching others ride, even if it was unlikely that he'd ever do so again himself. And it meant a great deal to him to be lauded by riders, that they should pick his particular organizations as the recipients of their money.

But in November he was back in the studio, imposing his vision upon all the footage running through the machines in front of him. At times what he wanted conflicted with the ideas HBO had for the production, which led to disputes, and he wasn't afraid to say so, even at a press conference to show the rough cut of the film.

"Chris was joking," recalled HBO NYC vice president Colin Callender, "because he was watching the film [on another floor]. He said to me, 'I'm quite sure, Colin, that you were up all night recutting the movie. . . . This cut you're showing upstairs is yours, while what I'm seeing downstairs is [mine].'"

However, in the end they had something that everyone at HBO was pleased with, and something that made Chris proud of the work he'd put into it. The next question was who would benefit from the premiere screening. Glenn Close had been in favor of Harlem Hospital, which she strongly supported, although Chris remained unsure. In fact, at that point he didn't even want to think about benefits. He'd attended enough during 1996 to say, "I'd gladly write a check for three hundred dollars to any group hosting a benefit, as long as I don't actually have to show up."

They were the words of an exhausted man. He'd spent the year driving himself as hard as he could, and made incredible progress along the way. He'd been determined to live as normal a life as possible within the limits he couldn't pass, and he'd done exactly that, flying all over the country, speaking here and there, attending shows, working.

What he needed was a break to recharge his batteries. He was still discovering things about himself, like the anger that he couldn't do the things he'd once considered perfectly normal, that he was trapped in a wheelchair, and still had to use his respirator.

Still, Chris must have been happy when HBO NYC announced that it would cosponsor two premieres of *In the Gloaming,* one in New York, the other in Los Angeles, both to benefit the Christopher Reeve Foundation. It was a natural choice, but Chris had neither mentioned the charity nor tried to prejudice their decision in any way. But more money in the research coffers was always welcome.

When it finally appeared on television, shown on April 20, 1997, the critics' reaction was mixed, as per usual. In *Newsweek,* Rick Marin stated that the script seemed "dated, as if nothing had changed since *An Early Frost* [the first movie on television to deal with AIDS] in 1985." *People,* while also citing *An Early Frost,* gave it a grade A, praising "an acting cast that plays this somber chamber piece flawlessly." And in *Entertainment Weekly,* Ken Tucker called it "superior to any domestic drama Hollywood has released in theaters in at least a decade," noting it was "the most ardent, vulnerable performance I've ever seen Close give."

And quite naturally, Chris's direction was bound to receive at least a mention. To *People* he deserved "credit," and *Entertainment Weekly* felt he made a film "intended for an audience that will appreciate the intricacy of its emotions." *Newsweek* found itself in the dissenting position on Chris's work here, too, stating, "Oblivious to cliches, Reeve directs this hourlong playlet through a sentimental haze, through the 'gloaming' of Danny's dying days. . . . That [Reeve] can direct at all is impressive. Too bad the movie isn't."

But it had been a difficult subject to deal with, something that had to be handled in an adult way. That anyone had been willing to finance such a piece was unusual enough, given that the only deaths America seemed to like on its small screens were violent ones. And to do it with someone who'd never directed before was a leap of faith, however much publicity it might bring in. Chris had performed remarkably well, enough so that more directorial offers in the future seemed inevitable.

For now, though, he needed to forget all that, to have a life again with Dana and Will, to think of himself for a while. He'd been honored and honored over the last year, and New York's mayor, Rudolph Giuliani, had probably echoed the sentiments of many Americans—indeed, people from around the world—when he spoke at "A Magical Evening," a benefit for the American Paralysis Association, and said,

"The courage, determination, and optimism with which Christopher Reeve approached his injury and recovery have been truly an inspiration to all of us. I think that a lot of his fans no longer idolize Superman, but we have come to idolize the actor himself as a real man who possesses the fortitude and bravery of a superhero."

One of the people there that night was one of Chris's acting heroes, Meryl Streep. For a decade and a half he'd continually sung her praises, to the point where, when she came over and began chatting to him on a plane, "I turned beet red. . . . I went to pieces. I started to sweat like I was eating curry."

She was the apotheosis of what he wanted to do in acting. Now he might never act again, certainly not in the way he once had, but he was still proud that she would attend this event where he was an honoree.

With Chris having shown what he could do, not only for himself, but also in support of the many victims of spinal-cord injury in the United States, so many people were happy to reach out and give what they could in return. In Princeton, his mother and others who'd known him when he was young organized "Coming Around Again: A Concert in Tribute to Christopher Reeve."

In many ways, this was the most personal of all the events that had been presented. It was to be held on January 20, 1997, at the McCarter Theatre, the place where Chris had received his start as an actor, and while it would feature big names, they were all people with a personal connection to Chris. John Lithgow's father, Arthur, had been the executive director of McCarter, and John had directed a very young Chris in a production of *Much Ado About Nothing.* Many Patinkin had been at Juilliard with Chris before making his name as an actor, and somewhat later, as a singer of distinction. And Carly Simon had got to know Chris and Dana when they'd spent time on Martha's Vineyard, where she lived.

It was a star-studded bill, and its aim was to raise $250,000 for the Christopher Reeve Foundation. But even those behind the scenes had their connections. The benefit chair had gone to school with Chris at Princeton Day, the concert producer had acted with him at McCarter. His great-aunt was one of the underwriters, and his mother was one of the honorary chairpersons.

By the time the event took place, the bill had been strengthened by singer Mary Chapin Carpenter, who'd been a hometown neighbor of Chris's.

"I guess a prerequisite to living in Princeton is that you have to be able to sing," Chris joked later.

And there was a very, very special surprise guest to round it all out—Dana Morosini, who appeared to sing standards.

Over eleven hundred people turned out for the show, paying between $75 and $500 for the privilege of attending.

For Chris it really was a homecoming, accompanied by Dana, two nurses, and a personal assistant. The occasion was emotional, with old friends coming out, people he literally hadn't seen in years. After a certain point it became embarrassing.

"My mother would say, 'So-and-so's coming,' and I'd think, 'How wonderful it'll be to see that person!' And I'd realize I hadn't done anything to make that happen in the past."

More than most public appearances, this one affected Chris. These were the people who'd known him when he was small, who'd seen him grow and been proud of him as he progressed in acting. While they could never know the pain he'd gone through—no one could, really—they'd been especially touched by his accident, and this was their reply.

"People have gone to such trouble for me," Chris said. "I'm grateful for it, but I get a little embarrassed." But he added, so obviously moved by the show, "If I never go anywhere again, this will have been enough."

But people weren't about to stop thinking of him, his own fight, and the fight he was conducting on behalf of all those other people. In May 1997, he received what was probably the ultimate accolade from the film industry, a star on the Hollywood Walk of Fame.

He attended the ceremony—how could he have forgone it?—with a broken arm, the result of sheer "bad luck" when he was dropped by two attendants moving him into his chair. But he was still firing on all cylinders, reiterating the cry he'd often issued for more funding for research into spinal-cord injuries.

"If we keep giving our scientists the funding they need for research, soon I will take my family by the hand and will stand here in front of the star," he said.

And every day it seemed a little bit more likely. In March he'd announced that he'd begun to regain feeling in his arms, hands, and back. The best thing about that was that he could actually feel when Dana or Will touched him.

He had, he said on CBS's *48 Hours,* sensation "all the way down to the base of my spine, which is really a big breakthrough, because to have feeling in the base of the spine is really important. About six months ago, I couldn't feel down there."

Excellent as that was, it still wasn't going to be enough for him. What he wanted above all was to be able to hold Will.

"That's what he's entitled to. That's what Dana is entitled to. And I believe that day is coming."

That Chris could still be so optimistic, almost two years after his accident, was a wonderful thing in itself. But it only highlighted the fact that he'd focused the fighter within himself, and put it to work on his behalf.

There was even the possibility of a real return to acting. Beyond a cameo in a television movie (*A Step Toward Tomorrow,* aired in June 1997), all Chris had been able to do on that front since the fall was his voice-over in *The Quest for Camelot.*

But now there was a vehicle that could prove to be the perfect comeback, as he was offered the James Stewart role in a remake of *Rear Window,* the Hitchcock thriller originally filmed in 1954. Tempting as it was, however, Chris didn't immediately embrace it with open arms. There was a small matter of the script. One thing he didn't want to be involved in was a simple rehash of what had been done before, however good it was. If the writers could come up with an original angle, then he would be interested, not before.

He was also taking the Christopher Reeve Foundation into its first business venture, as he endorsed a line of sportswear, the profits from which would benefit the foundation. If it seemed as if he was capitalizing on his name and public sympathy, then he was doing so not for personal gain, but to help the foundation, which meant getting more funding for spinal-cord research.

The clothes were aimed at the horsey set—caps, shirts, sweatshirts, polos, warm-ups—and all would have the logo of a horse and rider jumping a fence. To those who didn't realize, that would seem remarkably insensitive, but in fact it had been chosen by Chris himself, never one to flinch from fact or history.

With the collection priced on the high end of the market, the foundation had every chance of making good money, receiving either 20 percent of the wholesale or 15 percent of the retail prices of the garments (the sweatshirts were set to go on the market at fifty-five dollars each).

And in the middle of 1997, Chris received an unusually high honor, being named the vice chairman of the National Organization on Disability, putting him in an influential position to do even more good for those, like himself, without full mobility. In the two years since the accident he'd achieved so much and come so far.

And it was only beginning. . . .

CHAPTER FIFTEEN

If it seems that Chris has made miraculous progress since his recovery, that is because he has. Part of the reason is that he hadn't severed the spinal cord in the first place, a little was due to luck, some to the ministrations of doctors, nurses, and therapists, but for the most part the credit has to lie with Chris himself.

In refusing to just become another disabled statistic, he became an inspiration and a role model—not merely to other people who, through no fault of their own, were also in wheelchairs, but to everyone.

When he was in the hospital in Virginia, a picture of the space shuttle, autographed by its astronauts, gave him a focus, to be able to get up and aim for the stars. Now a picture of Chris, or an interview with him on television or in the press can have the same effect on someone else.

It would be overly easy to portray him as some kind of saint, who since his accident has dedicated himself to helping others through his speeches, his work for the American Paralysis Association, and his own foundation. But the truth is that Chris remains very human in his emotions. There's still plenty of anger and frustration that he can't move, that the things he can manage are limited. But it's all become positively channeled into the fight to regain control of his body.

And the work he's done has been as unstinting as anyone could expect from one person. Even when he'd rather relax at home—and every single day is a tiring regimen of physical therapy and exertion in one form or another—he's gone out and honored every commitment, whether it was for himself or for charity.

Even when he's had a full schedule of work, he's continued to give his time and energy to the causes that are important to him.

The accident changed his life irrevocably. Chris had always been a very active man, a skier, flier, rider, diver, sailor. He has the photographs of himself doing those things on the mantelpiece to serve as reminders.

"Much has been lost," he said. "But it doesn't serve any purpose to dwell on it."

There is a present, and most certainly a future, and those are the subjects he concentrates on—that he *has* to concentrate on. He has a loving family, whose support really has helped him through his crises, and as he regains movement, the idea of standing and then walking becomes even clearer in his mind.

But will he ever walk again? The doctors refuse to commit themselves, merely saying that it's still too early to tell. The one certainty is that if Chris has any say in the matter, he will. If it comes down to a matter of will, he'll be back on his feet. Those who complain that instead of campaigning for funding to find cures for spinal-cord trauma he should be crusading for disabled rights obviously don't understand him very well. While their point is understandable, Chris is fighting for what he believes in. Some people, because of the way they became disabled, will never get out of a chair, and they do deserve equal rights. But Chris represents those who might walk, for whom there is hope. In talking about it, he's raised the awareness of America with regard to the wheelchair-bound. But for as long as he lives, he'll battle to get out of his own chair and remain on his own two feet.

Every day brings victories and battles. Twice during 1997, blood clots have sent him to the emergency room. His family endured tense hours wondering whether everything would be all right each time. His entire life has to be monitored.

At home, a wing has been added downstairs to allow Chris and Dana something approaching a normal life. In a king-size bed they can sleep together, under the glow of lights, as machines keep track of Chris.

They've discussed the possibility of another baby, and would like one, but there are already three kids to be thought about. This year the whole family, including Matthew and Alexandra, went to Walt Disney World, their first vacation together since the accident, and one which took an entire year to plan because of Chris's special needs.

And when Dana needs to escape for a little while, she can sing in her car, or practice in her private soundproof studio above the garage.

For many, a Superman who was suddenly unable to move became the ultimate twisted irony. More than anyone besides an immediate family member, he could bring home to people how fragile the human body really is. If it could happen to *him,* then it really could happen to anyone. . . .

Chris had enjoyed the respect of many people for a number of years. He'd done the things that were important to him all the way through his career, all too often eschewing lucrative film roles to take juicy stage parts that he felt would challenge him as an actor. Yes, as even he admitted, he'd made some bad decisions along the way, which had caused his movie viability to go into decline, but they'd been *his* decisions, and he wasn't afraid to take the responsibility for them. Unlike so many in the entertainment industry, he behaved like an adult. Where he'd erred, he was willing to shoulder the blame, not pass it on to some hapless other person. He's always been a man in charge of his own life, who, in his early forties, had seemingly reconciled all the different facets of himself, a fully rounded and contented figure.

That, along with his articulate, thoughtful replies in interviews, and his other work, endeared him to people. He never went out of his way, for example, to highlight his trip to Chile, where he placed himself in danger for the sake of people he didn't know, or his activism on behalf of the environment. Those were things he did because they needed to be done, not to advance the career of Christopher Reeve. In many ways he'd grown into the perfect New England gentleman, not tooting his own horn, but going quietly about his business, and performing it to the very best of his ability, no matter whether he was faced with good or appalling material.

The accident made him a more public figure than he'd been in almost twenty years, and the outpouring of sympathy showed just how much people genuinely liked Chris. To people at large he was a movie star, but also a real person, more than just someone on the screen. He'd made friends, not enemies, in the business, and they, too, showed him what they were made of.

But to his eternal credit, he claimed nothing for himself, although he could have. Instead, he asked people to look beyond him, to all the other people with spinal-cord injuries. Chris could have isolated himself, concentrated solely on trying to walk again, worked, and let the rest of the world go away. People would have understood that, somehow. Instead, he did the opposite. He quite happily became a figurehead, pushing himself to the limit to address groups and raise awareness even though there was nothing in it immediately for him.

More people in America now are aware of spinal-cord injuries and what they can do than at any time before, and it's all due to Christopher Reeve. And the courage he's shown, both in his own trial to free himself from the chair and his willingness to work for others, has simply increased the respect everyone has for him. He is, in the very best sense of the word, a gentleman.

It's a shame that in his acting career—a career which definitely isn't over yet—he's found so few movie parts that really do him justice. But he was so perfectly cast in his first film that it was hard to go beyond that. It was a shame that so many of the things that seemed like good ideas ended up so poorly. Only in a handful of films was he able to show his potential; the rest were more or less just there.

Where he's always shone is on the stage. It's quite apparent, from the way he kept returning to it year after year, that his heart has lain there. The pay was nowhere near as good, but the satisfaction was much greater.

And for a while, Chris enjoyed the best of both worlds. He could really afford the lifestyle he wanted, be in a position to have his cake and eat it, too. Success came early, but it never went to his head. Indeed, by the time it started to fade, he'd achieved the kind of maturity he needed to be able to put his priorities in order. He's been a craftsman, a man in love with acting, both in its practice and ideas, for whom performing isn't confined to one thing. Whether it's television, audio books, whatever, he's taking part in the profession he cares about. He is what he always claimed to be, an actor, not a star.

He's also been lucky in his relationships. With Gae, he had someone who was supportive of everything he did, and someone who was a fully formed person in her own right, with a vital career of her own. At that stage, that was exactly what he needed. The kids they had helped keep his feet on the ground when it would have been easy for him to float on his own hype. They lived a good life together, with nannies and au pairs, but it was one that was well within their means.

With Dana, it seemed at first that he was simply going after someone who looked much like Gae, trying to replicate her. Instead, he found a woman who honestly seems to be his soul mate, whose love for him is unconditional, as is his for her. She, along with Will, has been his support, his rock, since the accident. She gave him the desire to live in those first few days. Their relationship has reached a new level, one that few get to experience. It continues to grow, and it was perfectly apparent to Barbara Walters when she visited the couple with their "true, shining love."

In spite of all the tragedy, Christopher Reeve is a lucky man. He has a family that gives him everything, and he's enjoyed, and continues to enjoy, a career that, for all its roller-coaster ups and downs, has offered plenty of satisfaction, with much more to come in the years ahead.

"My hope is for happiness, not for a cure," said Dana. "Chris hopes very much for a cure, but I just want a life that's full and joyful. Although there are tremendous strides in spinal-cord research, you never know. You never really know about anything."

In adversity he's had the chance to learn his own strength, and it's proved to be enormous. Christopher Reeve has truly become a superman, and though no one will believe that he'll fly, plenty, including himself, are utterly convinced that he'll walk again.

Patients have confounded doctors before, and determination can be very strong medicine. Chris knows what he wants, and he's doing everything he can to achieve his goal, not just for himself, but to try and give back to his family everything they've given him.

Really, it's only what you'd expect from a man who, even at the height of his fame, never wanted to think of himself as a star in the traditional sense, and was willing to become part of the ensemble—indeed, he was usually much happier that way—rather than be singled out. He did whatever was best and necessary for the production. And the production that is always at the back of his mind now is walking, to play with Will, to stroll with Dana.

His options as a professional may have seemed to constrict since his accident, but in many ways they've been opened wide. Now he's had the chance to direct, and quite successfully, an opportunity he'd been after for years, although no one seemed willing to take a chance on him then. There were a number of films Chris was involved in where he obviously suffered from bad direction; now he can make sure that doesn't happen to anyone else. And with his connections, his years in the acting profession, he knows the big names. They respect his body of work, his knowledge, and would be pleased to work with him—as can already be seen from *In the Gloaming*. Instead of his own performance, now he can shape the whole vehicle.

That Chris will direct again seems inevitable, given the right script. It's been a desire for too long for him to be sated by doing it only once. It keeps him involved, active, and that's important. And it brings in an income, which is equally important.

He's fought against the insurance cap as hard as he's fought for anything, but as yet he hasn't won. Soon his insurance will run out, which will leave him in a very difficult financial situation. Physically he's improving, but he still needs as much attention and therapy as he did before. Confined to a chair, his resistance to infections like pneumonia is lower. If Robin Williams does cover his medical costs, as has been rumored, but never confirmed, it would be a huge worry off his mind. If not, then he has another hurdle to face, and another reason to get out of his chair.

Will he do it?

If it's humanly possible, he will. Chris is not just a brave man, he's someone who refuses to accept the idea of defeat in this, or in anything regarding his life. He's showing us what people at their best can be, which is one reason everyone roots for him in his fight, and he deserves all the support we can offer him.

He's a gentleman, and a superhero. But above all, he's Christopher Reeve.

CREDITS

FILM

1978
Gray Lady Down
Superman: The Movie

1980
Somewhere in Time

1981
Superman II

1982
Deathtrap
Monsignor

1983
Superman III

1984
The Bostonians

1985
The Aviator

1987
Street Smart

Superman IV: The Quest for
    Peace

1988
Switching Channels

1992
Noises Off

1993
Morning Glory
The Remains of the Day

1994
Speechless

1995
Village of the Damned

1998
The Quest for Camelot
    (animated, voice of King
    Arthur)

THEATER

1976
A Matter of Gravity

1977
My Life

1980
Fifth of July

1981
The Greeks

1983
Holiday

1984
The Aspern Papers

1985
The Royal Family
The Marriage of Figaro

1986
Summer and Smoke

1987
The Rover

1988
Summer and Smoke

1989
The Winter's Tale
John Brown's Body

1990
Love Letters
Death Takes a Holiday

1992
The Guardsman

1993
*The Shadow Box (staged
    reading)*

TELEVISION

Love of Life
The Muppet Show
I Love Liberty
Celebrity Daredevils
Faerie Tale Theater
Vincent, A Dutchman
Anna Karenina
Juilliard at Eighty
Night of 100 Stars III

*American Portrait, Robert
    Goddard*
Dinosaur!
Future Flight
*The Great Escape II: The
    Untold Story*
*Superman's Fiftieth Anniversary:
    A Celebration of the Man
    of Steel*
World's Greatest Stunts

Valvoline National Driving Test
The Reporters
11th Annual Ace Awards
44th Annual Tony Awards
Black Tide
Road to Avonlea
American Tribute to Vaclav
    Havel and a Celebration
    of Democracy in
    Czechoslovakia
Carol and Company
The Rose and the Jackal
Things that go Bump in the
    Night
Death Dreams
The Road from Runnymede

Mortal Sins
The Last Ferry Home
A Stormy Night
Nightmare in the Daylight
The Sea Wolf
Frasier
Earth and the American Dream
The Unpleasant World of Penn
    and Teller
Tales from the Crypt
Above Suspicion
Black Fox
A Step Toward Tomorrow
In the Gloaming (director)